CHRISTMAS '01

<u>DAD</u>

FOR YOUR FUTURE JOURNEY
TO THE STATES.

LOVE

Fraser. and Susan xx

AMERICA

A USER'S GUIDE

AMERICA

A USER'S GUIDE

Simon Hoggart

With illustrations by David E. Smith

COLLINS · LONDON · 1990

Collins Publishers
London · Glasgow · Sydney · Auckland
Toronto · Johannesburg

First published 1990
Copyright © Simon Hoggart 1990

BRITISH LIBRARY CATALOGUING IN PUBLICATION DATA

Hoggart, Simon, *1946*–
America: a user's guide.
1. United States. Social life
I. Title
973.927

ISBN 0-00-215881-7

Photoset in Linotron Trump Mediaeval by
Rowland Phototypesetting Ltd
Bury St Edmunds, Suffolk
Printed and bound in Great Britain by
Hartnolls Limited, Bodmin, Cornwall

TO AMY AND RICHARD

Contents

Preface

America presents itself to the world, and to itself, as a bizarre and perpetually exotic country, a land of endless marvels and extremes. The middle-brow papers in Britain used to run columns of short, surprising items about the US under some title such as 'Dialling America'. 'Millionaire businessman H. Peabody Trufitt gave his wife the ultimate birthday present last week: a gold-plated Lear jet . . . in Oshkosh, Wisconsin, a dog robbed a bank.' But more serious writers have also tended to stress the miraculous, which they found round every corner. 'In Miami, fully one person in five is either a drug enforcement officer or a drug dealer . . . if all the wheat grown in Kansas were turned into bagels, they would stretch from here to the next solar system . . . if Vermont was a separate nation, it would have a bigger economy than the Windward Islands.'

All this was interesting, but what I found more fascinating when I went to work in the States was how ordinary people lived. The United States is indeed an astounding country, of tremendous size, beauty and prosperity – as well as comparative poverty. Yet the people who live there are not especially different from us. Their language, laws and religion are derived from ours. We often share the same names, watch the same TV shows and read the same books. While I lived in the States, I was only half-aware of being a foreigner.

Both our children were born there. When the first was coming my wife asked for an anaesthetic, which was administered by a Mr Gonzales, who came from the Philippines. As he worked over my poor, barely conscious wife, he chatted merrily away to me, like a barber. Where were we from? he asked. I told him England. A faraway look came into Mr Gonzales's eye. 'Ah!' he said. 'The old country!'

This book is not an attempt to ask what the future holds for

PREFACE

the United States, or to put the nation into the context of history, and especially not to seek the nature of America's soul. It is not meant to be at all comprehensive, and there are many lacunae in the coverage. Important subjects are left entirely untouched for no better reason than that I have nothing to say on the topic. My ambition was the modest one of simply recording some of what struck me while we lived there.

When I first joined the *Observer*, the editor, Donald Trelford, told me that he sent people to report from all over the world. When they returned, he would take them for a drink and they'd tell him amusing and revealing stories about where they had been. Then, he said, they got back into the office and wrote boring articles about Cabinet changes. He wanted, he said, a reporter who would write like he talked in the pub.

There are many other kinds of journalism, but that's a good definition of one worthwhile style. This book is really no more than what I would say to you if we were sitting in a pub and you had no means of shutting me up.

I owe thanks to many people: to the *Observer*, which sent me there and supported me and my family generously for four and a half years (as well as giving willing permission for me to use some of the material I sent from there in this book). Most especially I'd like to thank Adrian Hamilton, who was a constant source of warmth and encouragement, and Carol Keefer, our secretary in the paper's Washington office, whose efficiency and humour made the job of being a correspondent – and writing this book – so much easier than it would have been.

I'd also like to thank Jane Hill, my editor at Collins, and Natasha Fairweather, who realises that the most important part of an agent's job is to keep up her client's morale. And of course my family, for their considerable patience, their support, and for being there with me.

And finally to hundreds of Americans, some close friends, others just chance acquaintances, whose kindness and decency, and desire for us to discover and enjoy their country made our stay there some of the happiest times we have ever spent.

London, June 1990   S.H.

Introduction

I first went to the United States when I was ten years old. We arrived on the old *Queen Elizabeth* in 1956, the last year more people crossed the Atlantic by ship than by plane. In New York it was August, sweltering and humid. We waited for several hours in the great customs hall while my father tried to persuade one of the officers to clear our baggage. He thinks he saw people giving them money in the hope of getting an early escape. Finally he approached one, pleading: 'Can you help me? I have three children.'

'Don't ask me, see a doctor,' the man said. It was the first conversation he had with an American on American soil.

Nearly thirty years later I crossed by sea again, this time on the *QE2*. Seafarers are now the wealthy middle class – it's the poor who arrive by plane – so this time our customs officers were remarkably polite. One young woman cast an eye over our twenty-seven bags, packing cases and tea boxes, asked, 'You got any sausages in there?' and waved us through. It is one of the many curious misapprehensions Americans have about the British that we are addicted to our pallid, bread-filled sausages, and will do almost anything to smuggle them through, like a film star at Heathrow tucking a pet chihuahua under her coat.

Back in 1956, after that first unpleasantness in the customs hall I found that I liked America, a very great deal. Children do not love for particularly sophisticated reasons. The principal cause of my adoration was food. Rationing had only just finished in Britain, and though our family was well fed, like almost everyone else we had to be cautious because in England there wasn't a great deal of food around. Americans did not suffer from this problem.

11

They revelled in the stuff. They lathered it thickly all over your life. Great steaks, sides of beef, piles of brownies, hamburgers which would have made an entire meal at home, were guzzled down as a sustaining snack at a baseball game. Minor social events were accompanied not by a cup of thin English tea and a biscuit if you were lucky, but by vast beakers of milk and cookies the size of hub caps.

We lived in Rochester, New York, where my father was teaching for a year at the university. In summer, they gave a staff picnic, at which the children could consume as much fried chicken, ice cream and Coca-Cola as they wished. As much as they wished! For a small boy, it seemed an impossible romance, as unreal as an adolescent's dream of passing the night in a girls' school dorm.

Though I had been born a year after the war ended, it still seemed to be the central event in my life. In Britain everything people did was timed and related to the war. Fear that there might be another was endemic to my generation. Thanks to rationing, we were still, ten years later, living with the last vestigial privations. In Hull, where we lived at the time, there were still numerous bomb sites in the city centre. Nobody had enough money or enthusiasm to clear them and build something else. I assumed that these rubble-strewn acres were a part of every town centre, like the railway station and the department stores. The country seems, in retrospect, to have been curiously drained and enervated. Austerity matched the general mood. Men, in particular, were supposed to dress in as dreary a manner as possible. I remember being jeered on a football pitch at school because my boots had yellow laces. Now schoolboys have the opposite fear, of being inadequately flamboyant.

In 1949, a film star called Ronald Reagan had come to work in London, and had quickly decided that he hated the food and the weather. He had brought in steaks for his meals, but they were ruined when there was a power cut in the Savoy Hotel kitchens. He decided that England was a frightening example of socialism in action.

When I got there, America had pretty well forgotten the hostilities, or at least had put them tidily on one side. It was easier for them, for a very good reason: they hadn't suffered. Many families lost their sons and husbands, but nobody was bombed at home, and there had always been enough to eat. The war was not some crucial, catalytic event which affected everything that happened before or since; it was a blip, a hiccough, a pause in America's onward march. Most startling of all, they were quite clear that it was they who had won it on our behalf. We were indeed the plucky little Britain of legend, but had been helplessly outnumbered, doomed to defeat, and saved only by their magnanimity in coming to our rescue.

This was in bewildering contrast to the British view. Our doughty forces had held the line against Hitler; the Americans had deigned to come in only when the brunt of the struggle had already been borne. American troops, far from being the world's greatest fighting forces, were over-paid and over-sexed and not very good at what they did. The Yanks (nobody called them anything else) had the supplies and the manpower, but as soldiers they couldn't touch us. I suspect that this view, highly coloured and chauvinist though it was, may have had a glimmer of truth in it. Certainly the United States has suffered more than one military humiliation since the war, and its successes have tended to be symbolic rather than substantial.

(The term 'Yanks' is interesting. It was not always used contemptuously, but often with admiration, as in: 'The Yanks wouldn't mess about; they'd have it finished in a week.' In Third World countries it tends to be pejorative, as in 'Yankee Go Home'. But it would be even more offensive to use it against someone from the southern United States, to whom a Yankee is always a northerner. In the north it means a New Englander, and in New England usually carries an implication of upper-class English stock. In fact the term probably derives from 'Janke', a Dutch diminutive of John.)

The Suez crisis occurred while we were living in Rochester, and even at my age I could tell that this was one of those events which change everything that follows. American friends were polite, but evidently shocked. It was as if some favourite but dotty uncle had been caught robbing a store; they would hurry down to

13

the court and post bail, there would be a quiet word with the judge, but a harsher message would be delivered in private, at home. Suez was, I suspect, the moment when the American people finally realized that their country was now alone as the leader of the Western world; the head of the family, so to speak, obliged to take the decisions and cope with the responsibilities which go with that role.

I think there is still an undercurrent of resentment about this. Why is Europe so ungrateful? Americans think: we send our boys there to protect them against the Russian menace, or at least we did while there seemed to be a Russian menace. There was a spasm of considerable anger in 1986 when President Mitterrand refused permission for US Air Force planes to fly over France on their way to bomb Tripoli. The fact that France is not even in NATO was ignored; whose side were they really on? Why are the Europeans so damn pleased with themselves? We Americans don't *need* to be helping them; we only do it because it's our duty, heaven knows why.

The popular notion on the British Left, that the United States sees our island as little more than a convenient aircraft carrier, may be one way of looking at the situation, but it would be unrecognizable to almost any American. I used sometimes to give talks in Washington about how foreigners viewed America. If there were military men in the audience, their questions would often move elliptically round to asking: 'Why should we defend you people at all? What's in it for us?' We picture the Americans confining World War Three to Europe, prepared to see it destroyed in order to prevent nuclear missiles from landing on the United States. They see themselves sacrificing their men (and stationing vast numbers of troops and equipment there in the meantime) in order to preserve this less than grateful continent – which they have already rescued once and don't specially want to have to again, thank you very much.

Both views are partly wrong and partly right. Somewhere at the back of the American one, however, is the faint but still perceptible idea of their country as an unspoiled Elysium. From the squalid and squabbling states which made up Europe, many of the best people crossed the Atlantic to create from nothing a new and ideal nation. They succeeded triumphantly. Why should they be dragged back into the puny quarrels of the past?

And Europe is a terribly long way away. The great majority of Americans never go near the place. If you live in London, New York seems as close to you as it does to someone in Fargo, North Dakota. For one thing, more planes fly there. We have a vivid picture of New York in our minds which comes mainly from watching TV, exactly like the people in Fargo. In such places, almost everywhere can seem far away and irrelevant to your life. Politicians campaign around the country against 'Washington', which seems nonsensical, since that's where they spend their working lives. Yet Washington is an unimaginably long way off as well. It's as if we were to declare that we didn't want some bureaucrat in Kathmandu to decide how much tax we had to pay.

In Austin, which is where the main University of Texas campus is situated, I met a professor who told me that most of his students spent their vacations in Austin instead of going home. I said I was surprised, and he pointed out that, living in England, I had been raised within three hundred miles of London, Edinburgh, Paris, Amsterdam and Brussels. 'My students were raised within three hundred miles of grass.'

That sheer impression of size and distance has been eroded but not removed by the aeroplane. We can get some idea of how Americans see their world by picturing the early settlers, climbing the Blue Ridge Mountains in Virginia, around eighty miles west of the first ports on the Potomac River. From the ridge itself you can see an astounding distance, over the Shenandoah River, into West Virginia, almost as far as Ohio. For people used to the cramped lanes and hedgerows of England, it was the kind of view which would change the most fundamental outlook. Here it was, as much land as anyone could possibly need and, as it turned out, as much wood, as much coal, as much grass, as many minerals, millions of tons of meat on the hoof, to say nothing of the beaches which would later prove perfect for surfing and playing frisbee. Of course there were native Americans too, but, hey, who cared about them?

15

INTRODUCTION

If European politics in the nineteenth century was about dividing up the cake, Marxism was supposed to make the reallocation permanent. To the astonished Virginian in his buckskins, the idea must have seemed absurd. Everything you could possibly want or need was there, waiting for you, only provided you were prepared to cut it down, dig it out or plough it. That was the deal God had made: you could have it, but only if you did the work.

James Watt, Ronald Reagan's first, bible-thumping Interior Secretary, who held the opinion that if the Lord didn't like opencast mining he wouldn't have put the coal so near the surface, and that no seascape could fail to be improved by a few drilling rigs, was not a wacky aberration, but straight from the old-fashioned mainstream. Things have now swung the other way, so that in some National Parks they have laid boardwalks at 8,000 feet to protect the mountain from pedestrians.

The class system wasn't overturned by the Founding Fathers. It just wasn't relevant to the new country. Back in Europe it worked to keep wealth in the hands of those who already had it. Here there was as much wealth as anyone could need.

Naturally this happy state of affairs didn't last. The land was carved up at great speed, and the small family farmer is about to become a quaint anachronism like the occasional preserved log cabins which are still dotted about the West. But the sense of limitless plenty remains. The 'Green' movement in the US was for years way behind Western Europe, because the notion of 'holding back' was so unfamiliar. How could you tell people in a country where they buy gallon bottles of milk and cars twenty-five feet long that they ought to consume less? Now, however, the Americans have caught up with typical, manic speed and verve. A small example: in Boulder, Colorado, they instituted a competition for the best-sorted garbage. Keep your papers separate from your magazines, bottles apart from cans, and you may win a spot prize of a hundred dollars. There is an enviable panache about their enthusiasms.

I've always suspected that the overwhelming sense of abundance is behind the terror of Communism. Most Europeans think that it's a lousy system, because it plainly doesn't function. But

16

we can at least understand the theory. Americans don't even see that; since Communism is designed to handle a problem – the notion of limited wealth – which they don't recognize exists in the first place, then it must be not only flawed but somehow evil. The only way to greater wealth is through greater freedom, they would argue; a system which inhibits this process is necessarily corrupt.

At school in Rochester one of my classmates explained to me why Communists should be banned and preferably jailed. If not, he said, they might win an election one day. The implication was that this couldn't be through the democratic process, but only by necromancy. Such American Communists as I've met tend to be amiable, slightly loopy, herbivorous kind of people (though the more rabid ones seem to have followed their instincts as far as the neo-conservative Right, and now attack heresy from there in the same Trotskyite style they learned back in the Thirties). But this small band of socialists had to be hunted down as if by Torquemada. Since most Americans could not conceive any rationale for Communism, they tended to believe that no one could become a Communist by process of thought. It had to be infectious, and if it were not stamped out, it would spread like a plague.

The sense of abundance is everywhere. Near Fresno, in the central valley of California, one of the most fertile places in the world, you can drive past farms selling grapes for $2 a box, melons at $1 for ten. A reporter I met told me about his aunt from Chicago who had been puzzled by the absence of barbed wire. 'Don't people steal the fruit?' she'd asked. 'Why would they?' he replied.

Bizarrely, the feeling of plenty even extends to those who have nothing. Hope and possibility always remain. People do emigrate from the US, but not very many, and for the most part they are already well-established at home. They perhaps prefer the pace of life elsewhere, or some aspect of the culture. But almost no one else emigrates from even the poorest ghettoes. How many blacks from east Los Angeles do you see wandering round Brixton, looking for a better life? If they can get out they go to Phoenix, or New York, or Seattle. In America, emigration is almost always internal.

One underpinning of American life is the notion of 'American exceptionalism', a philosophy which grew up in the last century and, generally unspoken, still affects all America's dealings with the world. Put simply, it says that God must be on our side because we are doing so well. Listen to a speech by Pat Robertson, the TV evangelist who ran for President in 1988. I heard him at a women's clothing factory in southern Iowa where (as he presumably didn't know) they made the sexy stage underwear for Madonna, no relation. Robertson was specific. God would make America number one in the world again, but only when America returned to Christianity – by which he meant fundamentalism, not the milktoast teaching offered by the Episcopalians, the equivalent of the Church of England, which to the TV preachers is no more a religion than the worship of empty Coca-Cola bottles.

The crowd applauded in agreement. The idea that number one is America's rightful place was assumed, for these are the world's first self-selected Chosen People. You are redeemed by coming to America, or even by wanting to come. The collapse of Communism in Eastern Europe wasn't just seen as the rejection of cruel and incompetent dictatorships, but as the positive wish to embrace American values. Maybe they are right. When the Chinese students built a statue in Tiananmen Square they called it the Spirit of the Nation, but it looked like the Statue of Liberty in New York Harbor, and thanks to a confused translation, the American networks decided that that is what it was. It was an easy mistake to make. After all, people in Communist countries often paint their placards in English, and it certainly isn't because they're trying to get through to the people of Britain.

But one result is that Americans don't understand their opponents. Europeans expect to have enemies, whether Goths, Prussians or Argies. Americans can never figure out why they are hated, even by the people who lap up their television and their hamburgers. How is it that the very same Arabs who call the US 'The Great Satan' also love its TV shows? If J. R. Ewing went to Beirut, they wouldn't know whether to kidnap him or ask for his autograph.

In Bristol, New Hampshire, an idyllic small town in the White

Mountains, I watched the local Fourth of July parade in 1985. The parade's Chief Marshal was the then Vice-President of the United States, one George Bush, who seemed then a person of only marginal consequence. It was the time of the TWA hijacking, and from his podium, Bush waved a vague arm around the town. If only, he said, the hijackers could see Bristol, its people, its values; why, they wouldn't want to go about hurting any Americans!

Maybe so, and I could see what Bush meant. It was, I am sure, a wonderful place to raise a family, a place where the sense of community still meant something, where a family meeting hard times would have help from all its neighbours. I have no doubt that the churches of Bristol are full every Sunday, and its contributions to the United Way charity as high as anywhere in the country. I am not being sarcastic; these things are important and enviable. None of them, however, is any consolation to some peasant living in the Bekaa Valley who gets a Phoenix missile in his backyard. He's hardly likely to go dewy-eyed at the thought of the pilot's Mom helping in the Bristol bake sale or his sister selling Girl Scout cookies. America's warm, cosy and justly admiring sense of itself does not export.

Here's a more trivial example: when Reagan was to meet Gorbachev for the first time, his son, Ron Jr, suggested in print that the two men should start 'by throwing a football around'. But this would have been a uniquely American form of male bonding; Ron could not see that the Soviet leader would be baffled, and possibly insulted, by seeing a lump of leather spiralling towards him. Nancy Reagan would not, presumably, have been pleased if the Gorbachevs had hurled her crystal ware into the fireplace after drinking the toasts. But Americans tend to assume that their symbols of *bonhomie* are universal.

(It's a mistake all sides can make. In Washington one cold December evening I was one of a surly homegoing crowd being held back by the police at a street corner. After what seemed an age, a motorcade swept by and there, in the back of his Zil, was Gorbachev, waving in that come-hither manner favoured by the Queen. He clearly thought we were waiting to see him. He didn't realize that Washington is so used to celebrities that if the Grand

Vizier of Saturn were to pass by, few would look up, but all would resent the delay.)

It is the world's first manic-depressive nation. When I arrived to live there in 1985, the mood was of an almost chemical high. Grenada had been invaded, and this modest military feat was being presented as the first 'roll-back' of Communism. The United States had been overwhelmingly the most successful nation in the 1984 Olympics – admittedly in the absence of the entire Eastern bloc, but nobody paid much heed to that. Reagan had restored American pride, or so the Republicans claimed, and only a few malcontents and 'liberals' (soon to become a word of abuse) seemed disposed to disagree.

The climax of this particular manic spell came with the reopening of the Statue of Liberty on July the Fourth, 1986. Even those of us who love America found it hard to be as thrilled as Americans themselves. The sound of a nation slapping itself on the back was almost deafening. Hundreds of new citizens were sworn in at a mass ceremony, like a Moonie wedding. The festivities included a performance by scores of Elvis Presley lookalikes, a fitting symbol of America's greatness.

But by the end of that year the mood had become more sour. The Iran-Contra scandal made the country feel ridiculous, as its leaders had grovelled around in an effort to placate its bitterest enemy. The Democrats made the mistake of concentrating their attack on the illegal diversion of funds, and whether Reagan had known about it. This was to miss the point. What people found humiliating was the idea of trading arms with the Ayatollah Khomeini for American bodies. That is why they felt betrayed.

When America gets into one of its downs, everything contrives to make it more miserable. It's like the occasional depression most people suffer from; minor problems suddenly seem insurmountable. The United States began to suspect it might be finished, washed up. Books appeared, and were widely purchased, explaining how much better the Japanese did things. The most surprising bestseller of 1987 was a book called *The Rise and Fall of the Great Powers* by an English historian at Yale called Paul Kennedy. His point was that the empires of the past had over-extended themselves militarily, and that this had led to their downfall. He said there was nothing inevitable about this, and that it could, with forewarning, be prevented. But the Americans were too gloomy to hear what he was saying. Their decline was inevitable. The nation became like a pessimistic old invalid, unable to enjoy the sunny weather or its favourite TV shows.

Then the cycle turned again. The collapse of Communism in Eastern Europe was seen, as I have said, as a tribute to America and American values. The Soviets, having been hated and feared for forty-odd years (and before the war), became, for the time being, dear friends. Terrible, clunking Russian watches were a chic item in the more fasionable shops of New York. Former Communist countries were hailed with delight and admiration, and given anything they wanted, except money. Gorbachev was welcomed as an old and valued chum. The Russians must have felt that the United States was like a huge irrepressible dog: either it was running round you trying to bite your ankles, or else leaping up and licking your face.

The fear of Japan persisted, and had a nervy, almost schizo-phrenic quality. On the one hand, the Japanese were cheats, who refused to play on a level field. On the other – this view held with equal passion, often by the same people – they had got where they were by sheer hard work and a belief in delayed, rather than instant, gratification.

America usually sees foreign countries in terms of America. So it appears to them that the Japanese are sneakily overtaking the US by the underhand method of being unAmerican – corporatist in outlook, too closely steered by the State, too willing to surrender personal liberty. Yet simultaneously the Japanese are thought to be only affirming traditional American values, such as hard work and the sense of community, values which the Americans them-selves believe they are losing.

Once I was sitting in the Polish parliament waiting for George Bush to make a speech, the gist of which was, 'You have decided to become Americans yourselves, and we welcome you.' A Polish interpreter behind me finally got cheesed off with the constant drip of self-congratulation, and asked sarcastically, 'How many

American presidents does it take to change a light bulb?' We figured that the answer must be two – one to change the bulb and the other to declare it a beacon of hope and freedom.

'American values' are still widely assumed and still held in common. That is something most of us in Britain have lost, and many would think, a good thing too. But the sense of unity and purpose it helps provide is awesome. No country in the world is so vast and yet so unified. It is both utterly varied and entirely the same. A mechanic in Oregon and a clerk in Tampa, Florida, can wake up and switch on the same morning TV show, eat the same breakfast cereal, drive to work in the same car, eat an identical lunch from a nationwide chain, then at night relax with a dinner which includes the same brand of spaghetti sauce while watching the same TV shows. The weather may be different, but central heating and central air-conditioning make everywhere even feel the same temperature.

The homogenization of America has obviously been helped by the arrival of network TV (and before it the movies, and network radio), and by the size and efficiency of American commerce which oblige companies to expand until their product, whether cars or a new brand of extruded potato chip, can be found in every corner of the country. But a reverence for America and most of its institutions is an essential part of this process. Canada, by contrast, is an essentially fissiparous nation, where the west resents the east and Quebec dislikes everywhere else. But then Canada was saddled with the British political system without Britain's geographical cohesion.

The American Constitution is regarded in much the same way as the Holy Bible, and the unspoken sub-text of any discussion is that it too may have been dictated by God. (The most infuriating bumper sticker I can recall seeing read: 'Jesus Said It, I Believe It, And That Settles It'. Much the same view is taken of the Constitution.)

The Founding Fathers are spoken of with considerably more reverence than any other disparate bunch of politicians who have followed them. Since the Supreme Court has the sole job of interpreting the law in the light of the Constitution, many arguments

revolve around what the authors would have thought about telephone tapping, abortion and computer privacy, had they ever
conceived such things might exist. The citizen's right to bear
arms is enshrined in the Constitution, and is more or less the
entire case presented by the National Rifle Association for the
possession by American people of huge quantities of ordnance.

America's sense of self-esteem is impressive, even imposing.
I know of no country where the national flag is more commonly
seen, not only fluttering over public buildings, or proudly waving
on top of a used-car dealership, but outside ordinary people's
homes. Most especially on July the Fourth, but on plenty of houses
all the year round. On a bench in Delaware one August I watched
a large family group arrive and set up camp with beach chairs, sun
brollies and coolers full of food and drink. Then they took out a
thin, spring-loaded flagstaff about six feet high and Old Glory
flapped in the breeze, over their picnic.

What purpose could it have served? As a guide, perhaps, to
stranded submariners, who might not have known where they
were? (This is not quite so silly as it sounds. During World War
Two German submarines were spotted off Long Island. Were they
to reappear, like those forgotten Japanese soldiers, they would
take one look around the plump, luxurious towns known as the
Hamptons, with their qualities of Lowenbrau beer and Mercedes
cars, and assume that Germany had won.)

This patriotism and reverence for patriotic symbols can edge
into an unhealthy xenophobia. But usually it doesn't. Americans
are aware that, as a nation which created itself out of the people
of other countries, everyone is, in a sense, a foreigner. Europeans
tend to assume that you are what you are born; Americans that
you are what you decide to be.

The sense of endless possibility, the absence of limits, is
important and heady. When we first arrived in Washington, my
wife and a friend of hers decided to do some promotional work,
which neither had tried before, at least in the US. A small chain
of clothes stores was running a British Week and wanted to link
it with the imminent arrival of Charles and Di. They decided to
run a Princess Di look-alike competition, and started making

phone calls, more in hope than expectation. Of course, the British Embassy wasn't going to collude with such vulgarity, and British Airways dithered before saying no, but the American reaction was immediate. An airline gave two tickets to London as the grand prize. Someone else offered a week's lodging at a Chelsea hotel. A hairdressing chain wanted to be co-sponsor, and a bar handed over its premises for the night. Dozens of young women entered the contest.

Admittedly, some of them looked no more like Princess Di than I do, but the winner was marvellous. She might not have fooled Prince Charles, but she'd have got double takes from the waiters at Annabel's. Unfortunately it turned out that her job was to evict people who couldn't pay the rent, and she didn't even go on the trip to London because she was scared of terrorism. (It was a period when Americans were scornfully accused of cowardice by Europeans, though I wonder how we'd feel if there were anti-British gangs roaming the US, hijacking Greyhound buses and shooting any Brits on board?)

The contest was shown on three network television shows as well as local and foreign stations, and made quite a lot of money. It was pretty good for two newcomers, who knew they could never have done it at home.

Americans are always receptive to the possible. A friend's cousin in Mississippi was lent a million dollars by the bank to raise catfish for a firm which sells fast-food catfish burgers; which isn't especially surprising, except that he'd just come out from a year in jail. He didn't even know much about farming catfish. But he did expect to succeed. That familiar, drizzling sense of failure is largely unknown – even among people who fail.

A journalist I know was sacked, so he became a banker, and now has been offered the job of running the bank's Swiss office. A middle-aged friend in Florida, who had been a minister and an innkeeper in his past, found retirement dull, so he took up selling cosmetics door to door, and became his town's first Avon Man.

It does work both ways. Years later, across the street from the Lady Di bar, I saw a fable acted out which could have appeared in an inspirational essay by Horatio Alger or Samuel Smiles. A brand new BMW pulled up and out climbed four black youths, the oldest perhaps eighteen. They wore Italian designer trousers and 'box-fresh' Nikes which cost up to one hundred dollars a pair, and they sauntered with easy confidence into an Iranian-owned jewellery store, no doubt for some of that chunky stuff which looks like gilded hawsers.

It is possible that they simply had rich parents. Or it would be nice to point them out as an example of what you can achieve by hard work, delivering papers or shining shoes. But the money almost certainly came from the sale of crack cocaine, and the BMW bought at full list price from a dealer who didn't mind payment in crumpled twenty-dollar bills.

It's hard not to feel some sympathy. Anyone can accuse these youths of trading in human misery, but around the ghettoes of Washington there isn't a lot else to trade in. And they were only doing what America's most admired entrepreneurs do all the time: holding on to market share (in their case, by assassination, where necessary), avoiding the attentions of the police, giving the customer what he wants, and working dreadfully unsocial hours, from lunchtime until 4 or 5 a.m. the following day. They share with Wall Street the same love of greed and ostentatious consumption.

(This is not a knee-jerk belief that all crime is committed by blacks. The use of drugs follows quite closely the racial mix of the country as a whole. If whites didn't use drugs, blacks wouldn't sell them – or at least would sell far fewer.)

Americans expect to do well; they expect to succeed if they work hard, and they assume that no permanent barriers will be put in their way. It is that sense of limitless possibility which I most like and admire about America. There is a dark side, too. Mrs Thatcher, and her admirer Ronald Reagan, were fond of arguing from homilies such as 'you cannot abolish poverty by first abolishing wealth', or 'a rising tide lifts all boats'. It doesn't. The modern United States is, in some ways, a horrifying example of what happens when you decide to leave a large and discontented underclass to the mercy of market forces, ignoring their welfare, their education and their future. We are clearly making the same mistake here.

All that said, I remain bullish about the United States. Its astounding energy, its self-reliance, its extraordinary faith in itself, which continues even when the country is at its most miserable, and was there all through Watergate and Vietnam. It may have to learn that it is no longer the unquestioned economic giant of the world, but that will be no bad thing. Its powers of recuperation will see it through much worse than it has faced so far. The United States may not be, as Reagan liked to claim, 'the last, best hope for mankind'. But it surely remains the last, best hope for America.

ONE

Cities

New York is the only city in the world where I have been sworn at by a blind man whom I had just helped across the street. He wanted me to get him a cab, but there were road works nearby, so I had to step away to find one. 'Where der f*** is my cab?' he screamed. 'What der f*** happened to you?' Anywhere else in the world blind people find politeness the most effective way of enlisting help; in New York they have to be rude.

Elsewhere young Hindu women practise an elaborate, diffident courtesy. Not in New York, where an Indian bookstore clerk yelled 'Why the hell should I make change for you?' at the customer in front of me. The British writer Philip Norman, who used to live in the city, once told me that he would hoard his anger for each day, and spend it frugally, like a tourist husbanding his travellers' cheques.

I have a theory about this rudeness. It is my belief that New Yorkers yearn to be polite, but are terrified in case someone should find out. Stand peering at a subway map (most people could work out the formula for nuclear cold fusion in the time it takes to figure how to get from Grand Central to Penn Station) and sooner or later somebody will shuffle furtively towards you, whispering 'Need any help?' under their breath, as drug dealers mutter 'Smoke, smoke?' at you in such a way as to make their purpose plain without actually breaking the law.

A normal response would be to sob with gratitude: 'Oh, thank you, kind sir, I have been standing here for twenty minutes and I still cannot make out what these letters AAAA and B, Q, S, IRT mean!' This would be wrong. Your Good Samaritan would back away as if he were a member of the French Resistance and you an English agent newly parachuted in. Being rude is a crucial part of the city's *esprit*. The place may be dirty, crime infested and impossibly expensive, but by golly, when it comes to rudeness, they still lead the world. New Yorkers are convinced at bottom that if they are seen to be kind and helpful, the Mayor will send them back to Kansas, even if they didn't come from there. This is why they are the most surreptitiously polite people on earth.

For a New Yorker, not living in New York isn't the worst punishment it's possible to imagine. It's a kind of purgatory, or limbo, a sense of waiting, perhaps indefinitely, for the return. The city has a bigger diaspora than Israel, and there is a measure of guilt in all of them: 'If I forget thee, O New York.' In Washington we had plenty of friends who had once lived in the Big Apple (as absolutely nobody calls it). They used to sit in their lush, magnolia-infested gardens at the back of their four-bedroom houses and two-car garages, listening to the birds chirrup and their children play safely in the streets, wishing they were back in the magical city on the Hudson, sometimes abstractedly plotting their return like the Three Sisters yearning for Moscow: 'Next year in New York.'

If they were back, of course, they would inhabit some vile studio apartment in a converted 1940s asbestos warehouse with plywood partitions, a superintendent who doesn't speak English – but nevertheless is capable of following the sports commentaries on TV, which is what he watches all day, regarding any call on his time as a gross intrusion – a $300 a month bill for parking, and so many rodents that the mice have opened their own fast-food restaurant under the sink.

They would have all this for little more than it costs to pay the mortgage on an entire house in Washington or a mansion in Omaha. Tom Wolfe's novel *The Bonfire of the Vanities* is correct about New York, but wrong about how people outside the city feel about the place. The central character is obsessed by the notion that his Park Avenue apartment is the envy of the world. He's wrong. It's the envy of New York. In Dubuque garbage collectors have more living space – and somewhere to park.

In Washington, the first thing people tell you is what their job is. In Los Angeles you learn their star sign. In Houston you're told how rich they are. And in New York they tell you what their rent is.

Living in New York is like being at some terrible late-night party. You're tired, you've had a headache since you arrived, but you can't leave because then you'd miss the party.

New Yorkers adore the horrors and excesses of their city. In other places they boast about the clean air, or the schools, or the annual azalea festival. In New York they boast about the crime. When some particularly appalling event occurs, such as the unspeakable rape and beating of a young woman jogger in Central Park, they bask in the second-hand courage it awards to them. 'We can live here,' they seem to be saying, 'we can take it.' It's like the London blitz, every day. I noticed the same kind of attitude during the worst years in Belfast, a kind of swaggering pride. Even the upper classes can boast of fashionable street smarts.

Go to a dinner party in New York and the conversation quickly turns to the various crimes people have suffered. They should formalize it with medals. People would turn up looking like Ollie North in his uniform: 'That's for my three burglaries, and the oak leaf cluster is for the time I was mugged on the subway.' I met a young woman who had once been knifed in the street. It was the first thing she told me about herself – though it had happened two years before. Jack Nicholson gets it right as The Joker in *Batman*. Some politician promises to make the streets safe for decent people. 'Decent people shouldn't live here,' he says with that silky Nicholson leer, 'they'd be happier someplace else.'

It was the *Batman* comics which popularized the nickname 'Gotham City' again. This was coined by Washington Irving in 1807, in the satirical magazine *Salmagundi*. He was referring to the village in Nottinghamshire which was famous for a legend about its inhabitants pretending to be stupid, in order to dissuade King John from creating a royal right of way through the place. Irving meant to imply that the wits and wiseacres of the city were merely foolish, but thanks to Batman, the name has more sinister overtones.

There is always a fresh, imminent horror. It's round-the-clock goose pimples: the city's water system is about to break down, there will be a terrible drought, and no one will be able to shower for two months. Either way they win. If there isn't a drought, fine. If there is, they can boast about it all summer.

On the Fourth of July 1986, when they reopened the Statue of Liberty, the city traffic commissioner warned that the streets would be totally jammed. People who took out their cars, he implied, would be locked bumper-to-bumper for the entire weekend. They would have to eat and sleep in them. That Friday I found a cab on Third Avenue, and from Murray Hill, where you can see for about twenty blocks, there were four cars on the road. It was like a lithograph of the same scene as it might have been in 1910. Once again, New Yorkers had joyfully scared themselves silly.

They adore excess. Living in such an expensive city they have, for the most part, to be frugal, so entertain themselves with the lives of Leona Helmsley, Donald Trump and a host of other millionaires who selflessly delight the public with their gross conspicuous consumption. You can even share it. Anyone can walk into Trump Tower and feast their eyes on the peach-coloured marble, and the $3,000 dresses carried in the children's stores. I flew from Washington on a Trump Shuttle plane, while Trump still owned it, and the pilot was near rapture as he described the fitments Trump was about to introduce on his fleet. There would be 'leather seats, bird's-eye maple panelling in the bathroom, and marble vanity units'. Marble vanity units! The extra fuel required to lift them off the ground sixty-odd times a day could power a city the size of Dayton, Ohio! The extravagance, the needless expense! The bonfire of the vanity units!

When the financier Saul Steinberg turned fifty in 1989, his wife spent a million dollars on the birthday party. Among the entertainments were *tableaux vivants*, in which actors and actresses recreated famous paintings. The girl who portrayed Rembrandt's naked Danae had to keep the pose for four hours.

New Yorkers adore this kind of thing. In Britain they would be fascinated but they would hate it. In New York they realize that it is laid on for their benefit. So what if it cost a million dollars? The event provided the seventeen million people who live in the New York metropolitan area with far more than a dime's worth of conversation. In most other American cities wealthy people give a million dollars to the art gallery or the opera. Here they benefit the citizens by spending it on themselves.

Just as Americans find America quite as weird and intriguing as foreigners do, so New Yorkers regard New York as strange, bizarre and endlessly fascinating, For them there is a greater urgency. Nobody could possibly want to live there unless they regarded it as the most interesting city on the planet, since it most certainly isn't the nicest. So they need to tell themselves over and over again that it is spectacularly, sensationally unique. A woman killed in front of her own children because her husband was fighting neighbourhood drug dealers! A multi-millionairess who cheated on taxes by charging her underwear to the company! Rockefeller Center sold to the Japanese! Fully grown alligators roaming the sewer system! (Actually, that was a modern myth and entirely untrue, but so what? Which other city in the world can boast inhabitants who even *think* that their plumbing is full of giant reptiles?)

Every city needs something to persuade its citizens that it, and by extension they, are special, that their living in the town confers some cachet upon them. For most places it's the sports teams. New York loves its Yankees and its Mets, the baseball teams, and the football Giants, except that they moved out to New Jersey and, for sound financial reasons, are ambiguous about where their true loyalty lies. But they are less obsessive than, say, Pittsburgh fans or Dallas fans. Who needs sporting trophies when you have the most spectacular crimes and the most flamboyant millionaires in the world? In their own way, New Yorkers are as proud of Leona Helmsley as Denver folk are of John Elway.

This is why New York has two sensational newspapers. Other cities, such as Chicago and Boston, have tabloids – but none keeps up the constant fever pitch of New York's. 'Headless Body Found

In Topless Bar' is the most famous headline from the days when Rupert Murdoch owned the *New York Post*, but all conspire to offer the reader the prestige of living in the world's most thrillingly dangerous city. The *Washington Post* might label a story 'Drug Wars Claim Another Victim'; the New York papers offer: 'Junkies Shot My Mom'. You read this stuff each morning on the subway, where opposite the strap from which you are hanging are three derelicts who have been sleeping on the train through the night. One might imagine that the headlines add to the horror; on the contrary, they are the consolation for everything else.

WASHINGTON

Washington calls itself 'the most important city in the world', which may or may not be true. What is certainly the case is that it is best understood as a village. A very large village, to be sure, filled with imposing and important people, but nevertheless an enlarged version of 'Tilling', the name E. F. Benson gave to gossip-ridden Rye in his 'Lucia' books.

Washington has its own village 'characters', the equivalent of the postman and the local eccentric. There's our Fawn Hall, in the queue for the movie theatre! So pretty, but I'm afraid no better than she ought to be! And look, there's Senator Kennedy, just back from the pub, I'll be bound! And isn't that the celebrated Ambassador Paul Nitze, tucking into the paper-thin roast beef and sesame rolls? Perhaps you've never heard of him, but he is our 'wise old man', with a kindly word of advice for everyone. And that's Dr Henry Kissinger, the 'village idiot'. Oops, just my little joke, Dr Kissinger! What lovely weather it is, to be sure!

Of course, not everyone is as familiar with our local 'celebrities'. Once I pointed out to friends from Colorado Robert 'Bud' McFarlane, the former National Security Adviser who began Ronald Reagan's attempt to swap arms for hostages with the Ayatollah, and who later tried to kill himself. He was walking past our restaurant. My friends' reaction was quick: 'Who's he?' they asked.

As in Tilling there is a constant struggle for status, in which people's fortunes fluctuate almost daily. The principal setting for this struggle is the city's social life. A good speech in Congress, an admiring article in the *Washington Post*, our little 'local rag' – these can help. But they are not enough.

The British writer Tom Bethell once compared Washington to the pre-Revolutionary Russian army. This had two sets of rankings: the official ones, which applied in the field, and the real ones, which were what counted in the mess. Over dinner, a colonel would be inferior to a subaltern, if the subaltern happened to be the son of a count.

Washington's real rankings are a mystery to all but a handful of the people who study them – or rather who instinctively understand them. They could never be written down. They are simply absorbed. In the nominal, public order, it is the President who squats at the top of the totem pole. In the real pecking order, it is Mrs Katherine Graham, publisher of the *Washington Post*. We lived in Georgetown, a hundred yards from Mrs Graham's house, and when the streets were full of dark cars and men with earpieces, we knew that the President had been summoned to her table. She didn't put it like that. On the other hand, he knew better than to refuse. It is hard for people who live outside the city to realize how enormously important her paper is. When Mrs Graham had her sixtieth birthday party, the humorist Art Buchwald began his speech by saying that all her guests had one thing in common: 'fear'.

For example, the paper can destroy someone socially, or – to be more accurate – permit them to destroy themselves. When Arianna Stassinopoulos Huffington, the Greek socialite and biographer, arrived in town (it was Alan Bennett who said of her, 'She is so boring, you fall asleep halfway through her name', and Michael White who called her 'the most upwardly mobile Greek since Icarus') she came with impressive social credentials from both New York and Houston, which was her husband's home base. She clearly expected to take the town by storm. She failed. The *Post* ran a full-page interview in its 'Style' section. This is the beartrap it digs for newcomers. They covered it with twigs and a little earth, then waited for her to fall in. Which she promptly did, declaring that she fully expected her husband to become

President, and that she would consequently become the first Greek-born First Lady. Washington has seen and dismissed such hubris before. Mrs Huffington disappeared from sight, and soon her cars with their Texan plates were no longer to be seen outside the expensive Q Street house where she had lived.

The order of precedence is complex, and holds many hazards for the unwary. But up with Mrs Graham are Ben Bradlee, the editor of the *Post*, and his wife, Sally Quinn, who wrote a novel about Washington society in which one hostess awards points to her guests: five for a senator, four for a congressman, down to one for invitees who cannot be avoided. It's more complicated than that. Senator Alan Simpson of Wyoming carries much social weight, whereas his junior colleague, Senator Malcolm Wallop, has very little, in spite of his name. If you heard that a New York senator was coming to your party, you would pray that it was Daniel Patrick Moynihan and not Alfonse d'Amato. Simpson and Moynihan both pack more social punch than Dan Quayle, though naturally the Vice-President would be an intriguing curiosity, a conversation point. Everyone would hope that the Quayles left early so that they could talk about them.

Diplomats are unpredictable. Clearly the Soviet, British, Japanese, French and German Ambassadors have status *ex officio*, though this can vary from one occupant of the post to another. But the doyen of the corps used to be the Swedish Ambassador, and much the most celebrated on the social front was, for years, Allan Gotlieb from that distinctly unprestigious capital, Ottawa. Gotlieb was a most skilful Ambassador. As one of his friends put it: 'If he persuaded Ronald Reagan that acid rain isn't caused by trees, then he's worth every penny they pay him.' One reason for his effectiveness was that he knew everybody who really counted in Washington. He and his wife, Sondra, threw the finest and most lavish parties. Everyone attended because everyone knew that everyone else would be there. Each event was meticulously planned. She had her own witty column in the *Post*, satirizing Washington social life. The Gotliebs' downfall makes an instructive history. In Washington, success is just a training course for failure.

There were many people lying in wait. She was a trifle sharp-tongued. Some folk thought they recognized themselves in her column, and were displeased. Some did not, and were equally unhappy. Fellow diplomats resented their scant invitations to her parties. And beneath it all was an unspoken feeling that Canadians didn't deserve to be popular and amusing. Whoever next? New Zealanders? Norwegians?

Then one terrible night in 1986, the Canadian Prime Minister, Brian Mulroney, came to Washington. The principal American guest was to be the then Vice-President, George Bush, and the dinner would be the apogee of Mrs Gotlieb's career. In the end it marked the nadir.

Guests who hoped to be part of a small, exclusive coterie found themselves in a marquee, as if the entire party was an overspill. Experts on acid rain had been dotted around the tables, having the same gloomy effect on the environment as acid rain does on ancient forests. Mulroney arrived half an hour late. There was no sign of Bush.

Washington likes to eat early, and the assembled stomachs were rumbling. Mulroney decreed that no one should be served until Bush arrived. Mrs Gotlieb was in agony. To an Ambassador's wife, Prime Ministers are mere birds of passage. After he had returned home, she would have to face the *le tout* Washington, by now peevish, resentful and hungry. George Shultz, Secretary of State, arrived late, wearing a cream brocade tuxedo. Shultz was never entirely accepted by social Washington, and his decision to arrive dressed like the host of the Miss America pageant confirmed this collective view.

As she contemplated the disaster, something in Mrs Gotlieb snapped. She marched up to her own social secretary, and for no apparent reason, biffed her. This was no gentle tap on the cheek, but a beefy two-hander, slap slap!, hard enough to dislodge an earring, right in front of a knot of reporters.

A moment's loss of control, a lifetime to pay. Contrary to the speculation, the Gotliebs were not brought home to Canada – one of those countries where the capital and the equivalent of the Siberian power station are one and the same. He was too useful for that. But it could never be glad, confident evening for Sondra again. Her column was dropped from the *Post*, her social prestige dwindled to nothing. She was a victim of the diplomat's only fatal illness – 'canapé loyalty', the belief that your famous friends are more important than your Prime Minister. As for Bush, he did turn up, at 9.30. But by then he was fated to be, like Seyton in *Macbeth*, a walk-on character in someone else's tragedy.

Washington may be the last city in the world where journalists are almost revered. Any senior columnist is more important than most elected politicians. These days few people have the lapidary status of a James 'Scottie' Reston, a man who advised presidents, but any hostess would be proud to show off George Will, or William Safire, and R. W. 'Johnny' Apple of the *New York Times*. (I saw the power of this at work early on in our spell in Washington. I was chatting at a party to a man of medium importance who, when he deigned to look at me instead of over my shoulder, had that air which tells you, without it being actually said, 'You have exactly two minutes to demonstrate why I should spend any more time with you.' At this point the wife of a celebrated journalist, who had been a friend in London, came up and gave me a big wet kiss and a hug. From that moment on the fellow I was talking to stuck by me like a burr. My status had been established; I had been blessed by the gods, on a temporary basis, for that event at least.)

Most formal Washington dinner parties are roughly as casual as a court martial, though without the charm. Here is what happens:

You arrive on time; certainly, no more than five minutes late unless you have a very good excuse, such as needing to vote in the Senate, or appearing on certain TV shows (not all; Cable News doesn't count, for example, though the Ted Koppel show *Nightline* counts for a lot. But then you would usually have to leave early to appear on *Nightline*, which is almost the best possible way of bowing out of any function). Or you could try being straight off the plane from Moscow or Japan.

You are wearing a suit and tie, even if the temperature outside

39

is 95°F and the relative humidity 100 per cent. You are greeted by someone dressed as a butler, though it may well be that it's the first time he's ever seen the house. 'Raimundo is looking after coats,' cries your hostess, though since the air-conditioning has just dropped the ambient temperature by about 50°, you rather wish that he would fetch you one. Fur-lined.

A maid brings you a drink. Nurse it carefully, because it's the only one you'll get before dinner. Treasure those bits of ice at the bottom, because they still have a lingering flavour of gin. If you really need another, you may, *in extremis*, have to go into the kitchen and shout: 'Gimme a drink! I've got a grenade here! Fill this glass or I'll pull the pin!'

You will be served delicious nibbles, say an entire loaf of bread, hollowed out and stuffed with a dip of fresh artichokes, minced oysters, pine nuts and double cream. This is known as an appetizer, puzzlingly so, since it is so filling that you hope not to eat again for at least twenty-four hours.

There may be two tables, arranged so that nobody sits at the same board as their spouse. This simple and logical arrangement will not, however, prevent anyone from suffering the quintessential Washington fear: 'Am I at the "A" table or the "B" table?' There might be some obvious clues, e.g. champagne served at one, fruit-flavoured wine at the other, but almost certainly not. The whole and entire point about Washington status is that you don't need to have it spelled out, you just know.

The food is wonderful, culminating in a magnificent dessert of fresh berries, spun sugar, choux pastry and crème fraîche. But if it is served too late, then it is untouched, for at 10.30 sharp the ritual leave-taking begins.

This is as closely timed as the Greenwich pips or the swallows' return to Capistrano. It is never at 10.25, for that would be rude. Equally it cannot be at 10.35, for that would affect the status of the guests. Neither can anyone say: 'We have to go now, we want to be in bed', or even, 'We have to go, it's half-past ten.' You must have an excuse, and the more exotic the better. Indeed, your reason for leaving is probably the most important status indicator of the night. These would serve very well:

'Oh my, is that the time? My tennis game with the Secretary of the Treasury is at six o'clock tomorrow morning!'

'Why, goodness, I really need to go. I have a top secret flight to Tehran tomorrow and I still haven't picked up the cake!'

'Heavens, we must leave! Our sitter is a reformed axe-murderer, and we really do need to check on the kids.'

At this point your hostess, who has spent the whole day slaving over a hot Filipino, looks baffled and distraught. Do not be fooled by this. It does not mean that you should stay. Even if she pleads, 'Must you go?' the correct answer can never be, 'Well, a large brandy certainly wouldn't come amiss.' Instead you must say: 'I'm afraid not, the White House Situation Room waits for no man!' Staying on will not only keep your host and hostess out of their own bed, but will brand you as a person of no consequence, whose life is so empty and meaningless that you have no need to be awake again at dawn.

LOS ANGELES

There is a place called Los Angeles, though you don't often meet people who live there. It has a population of under three million, many of whom live in conditions of squalor and misery. Together they constitute less than a quarter of the population of the greater Los Angeles area, which is probably the most majestic urban sprawl in the world. Depending on where you precisely draw the line, it stretches for roughly a hundred miles in every direction. There are several countries which occupy less land than Los Angeles.

This is all linked by the celebrated system of 'freeways', a demented cat's cradle of roads, some of them twelve carriageways wide, some stacked on top of each other, waiting to collapse in an earthquake. There are two speeds which apply on the freeways, depending on the time of day: dangerously fast, and stationary. This is what it's like joining a freeway when the speed is set at 'fast':

You drive up a ramp, where there's a small traffic light labelled 'One car per green'.

You wait for your light, then advance towards the freeway itself, where there's another sign saying 'Merge'.

You merge in the fashion that Belgium merged with Germany in 1914; it is an entirely one-sided process. What you see is six lanes of cars, all driving well above the 55 m.p.h. speed limit, but bumper-to-bumper nevertheless.

You are supposed to find a gap in the 'slow lane' (i.e. the one in which the traffic is travelling at only 10 m.p.h. above the limit), and fill it. Except that there are no gaps.

Over the years of visiting Los Angeles I discovered a sophisticated, foolproof technique for dealing with this problem. I closed my eyes, swung the wheel to the left, and prayed.

Once you are in the mainstream, driving has a certain dream-like quality, a stillness even at speed. Cars weave lazily in and out of the lanes, sometimes missing your front bumper by a few feet, which wouldn't much matter in a parking lot, but ought to be scary at 75 m.p.h. Yet somehow it isn't; you feel as if you are a part of a single vast articulated serpent. It's a little like being a Scientologist; your individuality is lost in the general will.

Of course in the 'rush hour' the sense of stillness derives from the fact that you *are* completely still. This period has been steadily extending itself, and now runs from around 7 a.m. to 11 a.m., then from 3 p.m. until 8. One afternoon I tried to drive from the centre of Los Angeles to Irvine, on the edge of the metropolis, about forty miles to the south. It took three and a half hours. At one point, where the road climbed, I was able to look down on perhaps a thousand cars spread over twelve lanes, around ten million dollars' worth of transportation doing no transporting at all.

No wonder that American cars are designed to keep the outside world at bay. European cars demand lots of fussy attention; you are forever having to change gear or wrestle with the steering wheel. The suspension is highly sprung, so that the state of the road beneath you is directly transmitted to your coccyx. American suspension gives you a soft, pillowy ride, so that even on a pot-holed road, you feel as if you are in bed – and are in much the same dreamlike trance. You rarely change gear; power steering means that the half-sensed perception that you need to change direction merges with the physical action. In an American car the mind has complete control over the body. Think that you wish to swing left, and magically the car goes left. Air-conditioning and tinted windows keep the weather out, so that you might be in a bathysphere, gliding gently, imperceptibly along. The difference between great speed and a dead halt is hard to discern.

The sense of surrealism is heightened by the fact that one of the star presenters on the leading Los Angeles talk radio station is a South African called Michael Jackson (also no relation). Jackson has a faultless, wonderfully modulated English accent of a type which you ceased to hear in England decades ago. So there you are, sitting in your car, while forty-foot long eighteen-wheelers, giggling bearded crazies drinking beer in beat-up old pick-ups, and sinister men in dark suits and tank-sized Mercedes roar past you, while a Wilfred Hyde White sound-alike is murmuring politely, as if in his club, 'Might we legalize drugs?' or 'Should homosexuals be allowed to adopt children?'

The most famous district of Los Angeles is, of course, Hollywood. This has fallen on hard times. Walk down the famous Sidewalk of the Stars and learn about the transitory nature of fame. Along with Laurence Olivier, Walt Disney and Marilyn Monroe are Scatman Crothers, William Lundigrans, Mabel Taliaferro, Ford Bond, J. Peverell Marley, each metal star as vivid a symbol as the headless trunk of Ozymandias. Outside Graumann's Chinese Theatre the tour buses still wait, but the streets around it are suffering from a peculiarly glamorous form of urban blight. Hoboes beg for change, the only other cinema nearby is showing porn (*Space Vixens* – 'They've come to suck your fluids' when I last visited), and the principal attraction is the Bra Museum at Frederick's of Hollywood (q.v.). This contains bras worn by Mary Wilson of the Supremes, Madonna, and Tony Curtis in *Some Like It Hot*. Phyllis Diller's is wittily marked 'This side up'. A few blocks away young Hispanics deal in drugs, more or less openly.

Los Angeles is still the world centre of the entertainment industry, but the stars are spread more thinly now. The break-up of the old studio system, the smaller number of movies being

43

made, and the fact that they can be filmed much cheaper elsewhere – in Canada, Europe or almost any other American city – means that the stars don't need to live there any more. Some still do, but others, such as Robert Redford and Michael Caine, prefer to be elsewhere. Woody Allen despises Los Angeles and won't even turn up for the Oscars.

The tourists still take bus tours of the stars' homes. You can always tell the richest neighbourhoods in America by the crummy, rusting vehicles parked outside. These belong to the gardeners and maids. The Porsches are parked indoors. These days the great mansions are more likely to be occupied by lawyers, producers, accountants and retired politicians. Ronald and Nancy Reagan live in a relatively tiny dwelling at 668 St Cloud Avenue in Bel Air, a house worth a mere 2.6 million dollars when it was bought on their behalf, less than half of what a typical property in the area would have cost. They had the number changed from the original '666', which is, as is well known, the Mark of the Beast in the Book of Revelations. Reagan, being a part-time believer in Armaggedon theory, would naturally not want a Mailbox From Hell in his driveway.

The Reagans' house is uncomfortably close to the road, and even closer to the swimming pool, or 'cee-ment pond', which was used for the TV show *The Beverly Hillbillies*, a fact which to some of the bus-borne visitors is quite as interesting as the home of the former President. But Hollywood's days of glory are probably gone. One of the most popular modern attractions is a trip run by Greg Smith, who used to be an undertaker in Kansas, and who now runs 'Grave Line Tours', a two-and-a-half hour ride round the most ghoulish attractions in the area. In a rebuilt hearse he takes visitors to see the house where Sharon Tate met the Mansons; the place where Lana Turner's boyfriend was murdered by her daughter; the motel where John Belushi overdosed – 'He checked in, but he never checked out,' says Smith. We see the Hollywood sign, where the English actress Peg Entwhistle died after throwing herself forty feet from the letter 'H' after RKO declined to renew her contract. The whole trip has the sweet and rotten smell of death and decadence, a little like Hollywood itself.

These days the stars live further out. An hour north along the Pacific Coast Highway is Malibu, perhaps the best known of all the colonies where these exotic specimens nest. Does Malibu really exist? Even when you're there it's hard to be certain. In the late afternoon, the low sun shines through the permanent spray from the sea, making the whole town glow gorgeously orange as if it had been filmed on faded Technicolor stock.

There are huge houses, imitation Spanish missions, Rhineland castles and stockbroker Tudor, perched improbably on the canyon cliffs over the town, as if they had been painted on the backdrop of a comic opera. Placards of the burglar alarm companies make each front garden a riot of colour. The most prestigious houses are, however, on the private beach. If you have one of these you must share your patch of sand, but only with others who are as rich and famous as yourself.

The inhabitants looks as unreal as their town. Even the garbage men have the veneer, the posture and the gait of true celebrities. Folk in Malibu aren't merely tanned; they are french polished. They could be described like expensive chocolates: 'Mr Strumberg is lightly glazed, lovingly encased in silk lounging trousers, and topped with a creamy sweater made from the pubic hairs of angora rabbits.'

Malibu folk like to tell you that it's really just another American small town, which is like calling the Pope just another priest. Few small towns anywhere else are home to the likes of Barbra Streisand, Sylvester Stallone, Larry Hagman, Martin Sheen, Whoopi Goldberg, and America's highest paid TV entertainer, Johnny Carson. Ms Streisand's compound alone cost 20 million dollars. One reason celebrities like the place is that they can keep some measure of privacy – or at least pretend to. In Malibu the town's self-esteem – the equivalent of New York's rudeness – demands that you never raise an eyebrow if someone famous walks by. A teacher I met said: 'It would be just so tacky to act all excited if you saw Ali McGraw in the supermarket. But when you get home, you can't wait to let everybody know.'

I ate in the La Scala restaurant, which probably has more famous people among its customers than any other establishment in the conurbation, but a lot fewer rubber-neckers since it's so far out. It does orders to go as well, making it possibly the world's most upmarket takeaway. There was a terrific buzz when a star walked in. It turned out to be Burgess Meredith, of whom I hadn't actually heard, but who apparently played Sylvester Stallone's manager in Rockies I through IV. Our waiter quivered with excitement: 'And who did you spot tonight?' he asked. The sense of wonder which critics find in American literature never leaves American people; no familiarity is too great to dull it. I felt like my Colorado friends who didn't know who Bud McFarlane was; like McFarlane, Burgess Meredith is world famous in his home town.

Mind you, the people I was having dinner with were on the fast track to becoming celebrities themselves. I first knew the husband when he was just another struggling playwright. Now he writes scripts for Michael Douglas. Scriptwriters are still regarded as the untouchable caste in Los Angeles; there's a harsh joke about the Polish starlet who sleeps with the writer. But working for Douglas is the equivalent of having a job in the White House which gets you into the Oval Office at least once a year. Possessing, say, one hundredth of Michael Douglas's fame is to be extremely important yourself; in Los Angeles, celebrity can be acquired on a percentage, commission basis.

HOUSTON

Houston is about to become the World's Greatest City. This is not a view shared much outside Houston, but then if you live in Houston, you don't care an awful lot about what anyone who doesn't share that good fortune thinks in the first place.

Consider the evidence. The President of the United States comes from Houston (well, he doesn't actually, but he likes to claim that he does, and so far as Houston cares, that's quite enough). So do his Secretary of State and the Secretary of Commerce. And, more to the point, so does the Secretary of Commerce's wife, one Georgette Mosbacher, who made her money selling a beauty treatment made from the placentas of Swiss sheep.

When she returned to Houston after attending the President's inauguration, kind friends asked: 'Did you take Washington by storm?' 'That's what I hear!' she cried.

Even the President's dogs are named after prominent Houston citizens. For example, 'Millie' is named after Mildred Kerr. This makes Houston the only city in America where to be called a bitch is a mark of social distinction.

The first word uttered on the Moon was 'Houston', as in, 'Houston, the Eagle has landed'. Only a Houstonian, finding it too hot and sticky to watch baseball outdoors in summer, could decide to build the Astrodome, which was the world's first indoor stadium. When Prince Rainer came to Houston, the Mayor asked if he would like to have an Astrodome in Monaco. 'Yes,' said the Prince, 'in that case we would have the world's first indoor country.'

In the 1980s, Houston faced its first ever slump. When I went to visit the city towards the end of the decade, I found people much cheerier. Property prices were bouncing back, and a house in River Oaks, quite the poshest part of town, was on the market for 35 million dollars. The realtor who was dealing with it said: 'I do admit that this property might not reach its full asking price. It does not have a fireplace, and for thirty-five million dollars you *expect* a fireplace.' I mentioned this to a Houstonian friend, who did not sound at all surprised. 'Daddy loved a fire,' she said. 'Of course it meant that he had to keep the air-conditioning on full.' Of course. In Houston, nature knows its place.

Fish have water, the bushmen of the Kalahari have sand, and Houstonians have interior décor. In 1949 an oil man called Glenn McCarthy opened the Shamrock Hotel, which looked like how an Irish contractor might have designed the Taj Mahal. He used 63 different shades of green on the inside alone. He invited 175 Hollywood stars to the opening, plus Frank Lloyd Wright, who looked at it and uttered the one word: 'Why?' Later, he added: 'I always wondered what it was like inside a jukebox.'

Of course the Shamrock was knocked down a long time ago. Houston is always re-inventing itself. Before the oil boom went bust, the fashion was for the most adventurous modern architects.

So the downtown skyline is sensational, smaller but more exciting than New York's. Here is an Aztec temple, there a black twin-trapezoid, now fifty storeys of reflecting glass, like a gigantic Zippo lighter.

In the city's most famous restaurant, Tony's, the décor is composed of luridly lit reproductions of Old Masters. Tony's has the use of a helipad, so that customers don't have to waste time in their cars. A popular rival is the Confederate House, which serves southern food to people who could easily afford the finest French cuisine, but prefer the dishes of their childhood. The décor here is portraits of Confederate generals on one wall, and a *trompe l'oeil* view of a Tara-like plantation on the other. The waiters, mainly black, have the casual grumpiness of old, well-established family retainers. It all fantasizes that the Civil War is over, but this time the right side won.

At the Confederate House I enjoyed a bottle of Texas Chardonnay wine, which does not sound like the kind of tipple the boys in the boots would drink. Yet there is a substantial yuppie element in the city now, and a large gay community. It also has a woman Mayor and a black Chief of Police.

The first inhabitants of Houston were probably English settlers, who arrived in 1631. They were identified from their graves, which were of a type invented in London shortly before. It's nice to imagine how things might have worked out if they had stayed: posters advertising 'World's Biggest Cucumber Sandwich' perhaps, or cricket in the Astrodome. In the end they vanished, probably to the West Indies. I asked Dr Kenneth Brown of the University of Houston, the man who discovered the site of their settlement, why they had failed. 'This was a totally alien environment for them,' he said, 'a hot, swampy, mosquito-infested place. What they suffered from was Culture Shock.'

This has remained a problem ever since the city was founded in 1836, by two New York hustlers who had bought the land and advertised it back east as an undiscovered paradise. In fact, it was built on swamp and surrounded by alligators. However the brothers hit on the excellent PR scheme of naming it after Sam Houston, the general who defeated the Mexicans after the Alamo.

48

For years the citizens survived on trade, commerce and thieving from each other. Houston's nickname is 'Baghdad on the Bayou' and the evangelist Billy Graham once remarked: 'Most Houstonians will spend an eternity in Hell.'

Oil, first discovered in 1901, is what brought the likes of George Bush out to Houston, where he could play at being a rough, tough wildcatter in the way that Marie Antoinette used to play at being a shepherdess. Bush is in the habit, whenever he fears that his Texan credentials might be in question, of hitching up his boots on to a nearby table and making some tangled remark along the lines of: 'Don't never let them tell you George Bush is not a Texan!'

Houston people give huge sums of money to worthy causes, especially to the various 'disease balls' and to the arts. This is why the city has an opera house of almost the first rank, and galleries such as the Menil and the Rothko Chapel, which exhibit the toughest modern art. There is no middlebrow fluff here. Most Houstonians willingly admit they don't understand it, but they do understand that it is the very best in its field, and nothing less could possibly suffice.

I was invited to a black-tie gala at the Houston Country Club (favoured by George Bush and the Secretary of State, James Baker). It was in aid of the Costume Institute, a lavish museum of dress, and the guest of honour was the severe New York designer Donna Karan. She was dressed as if to appear in court on a charge of murdering her husband. In this she was alone. Brocade, velvet, satin and shantung: that was just the men's vests and cummerbunds. The women were not just dripping with diamonds; they seemed to be held up by them, like exoskeletons. When they danced, their jewellery flashed back, a thousand points of blinding light.

Back east, of course, people don't usually wear all their jewels at the same time. They tell of one Houston *grande dame* who was told politely: 'In New York, you just don't wear so many diamonds, especially in the daytime.' She smiled back: 'I used to think so too — until I had them.'

Houstonians talk in vivid quotes. Of a woman who drank too

much: 'We all want to be reincarnated as her liver.' Two women of a certain age regretting a lack of variety in their love lives: 'Here in Houston, there are only three types of men: married, gay and pond scum.'

It's an inclusive society. New people are always welcome, especially if they have a lot of money. They are encouraged to seek out the services of a public relations man, such as Hal Foster, who will explain exactly which balls to attend and so which charities and artistic undertakings you should support. Imagine the horror of paying 25,000 dollars for a table, which you can easily do, and nobody paying any heed! Luckily Foster's dear friend is Betsy Parish, the social columnist of the *Houston Post*. A mention in her daily column is not only the equivalent of the Royal Warrant but a sort of metaphysical proof that you exist. It doesn't matter terribly just what Betsy writes. The fact that she writes it proves that she came, and, *ergo*, your party was a hit.

The Johnson Space Center is near Houston. It is magnificent, of course, but it also has a faintly dated feel now, like Billy J. Kramer records and mini-skirts. No man has stepped on the moon for nineteen years. Why did we want to go in the first place? At the Space Center you can wander round and see, along with the impressive hardware, intriguing items such as the Velcro-covered darts and dartboard which the astronauts used to entertain themselves on long missions.

In the old days no party worth a mention in the social columns was without an astronaut who, like the Saudi Royal Family, were seemingly innumerable and yet socially essential. Contrary to their cultivated image of clean-cut, decent, American young men, they were noted hell-raisers, and their idea of fun on *terra firma* had nothing to do with Velcro-covered darts.

These days bankruptcy and murder are two of the principal social events. When the big bust came in 1986, for the first time oilmen were replaced as the largest single group living in River Oaks by lawyers, many of whom had handled the oilmen's bankruptcies. When John Connally, the former Governor of Texas, went belly up, the auction was listed in the social 'Black Book' and people came to the event wearing their finest clothes. Kind friends paid a fortune for geegaws, such as a 15 dollar eggtimer which went for 850 dollars.

Houston has probably the most advanced hospitals in the world, and doctors are great social climbers. Dr Denton Cooley is one of the world's celebrity heart surgeons. His medical skills made him rich, which won him a place in Houston society, obtaining him more patients, and making him richer still. Then he went and spoiled it by investing in real estate, so that when the slump came he went bankrupt, filing debts of some 99 million dollars, which is slightly more than even an American GP expects to earn in his whole lifetime.

Luckily the bankruptcy laws in Texas are lenient, and he could keep his home, plus 30,000 dollars in personal goods – priced not at their value but at what they would notionally fetch at auction, a loophole which allows some bankrupts to salvage the Rolls. In Houston, you are what you keep.

The city loves its great rococo murders. These are not the squalid muggings of New York, but elaborate marital affairs, Agatha Christie on the Bayou. Some are straightforward. Joan Sandiford shot her husband in the back one night, while he was armed only with a copy of *Time* magazine and a milky drink. Juries are lenient on such peccadilloes, so she got a probated sentence and never went to jail. Also, nobody liked him anyhow, so they held a celebration barbecue when she was released. Sandy Sheehy, who wrote a book about the city's rich, says: 'The thing about Houston is that you can murder your husband, and still get invited to the right parties afterwards.'

Houston juries generally convict for theft, but acquit for murder, thus showing a fit, Texan sense of priorities. Houston lawyers are thought to have almost magical powers. The late Percy Foreman, a vast man whose nose alone looked like an advanced case of cirrhosis, was the most celebrated. He was once asked in court if he made a practice of bedding his female clients, and replied: 'Why, they expect it of me.' A friend once inquired if he wasn't concerned that some of his clients might be guilty. 'Honey,' he said, 'if they ain't guilty, they don't need Percy Foreman.'

His flamboyant successors include Richard 'Racehorse'

51

Haynes. 'If you're going to murder your husband or wife,' Haynes once said, 'the place to do it is Texas.'

Not long ago Haynes attended a fund-raising dinner auction. Though the prizes included such items as a Caribbean cruise, some women were so inflamed by his presence that they started bidding on his socks, which fetched 200 dollars. Then he arranged for himself to be modestly surrounded by friends, and sold his own jockey shorts, on the spot, for 500 dollars. The most extraordinary thing is that the fund-raiser was for a judge who was seeking re-election. Only in Houston would an attorney seek to curry favour with a judge he might have to face in court by taking off his underpants and selling them in public.

SEATTLE

You can chart the yuppie migration across North America. It would look rather like those history maps at school, which show broad arrows indicating the Saxons on the move west, or the Visogoths *en route* for Rome. Ten years ago the yuppies swept into the Sunbelt bringing craft boutiques and mesquite grilled chicken satay to the puzzled, and occasionally resentful, inhabitants of Key West, Houston and Phoenix. Sometimes they established their own yuppie communities in places like Sedona, Arizona, where nobody had done much for years except punch a few cattle, whatever that might mean. They are now filled with New Age music, peculiar cults whose members believe in reincarnation, handmade silver and turquoise jewellery, and enough fresh basil to cover Birnam Wood's advance on Dunsinane. Like the Moors in Europe, they left the marks of their culture everywhere. Like the Beaker Folk they could be identified by their utensils: the Le Creuset Folk perhaps, or the Ozone-Friendly Styrofoam Cup People.

Now the yuppies are on the move again, and their caravan of Volvos and Subarus is headed north-west to the Rain Belt, or 'Burberry Coast'. Specifically they have picked Seattle, a spectacular city of hills and water in the top left of the country, hard up against the Canadian border.

Naturally the locals gripe. Usually new immigrants are accused of forcing property prices down, though these have pushed them up, which appears to be an equally serious offence. For some reason they especially hate Californians, and of Californians, they specifically detest Los Angelenos, who are heading north in their thousands. Who wants to live in a city where you can *see* what you are breathing? They discover that they can buy a small mansion in Seattle for what their sleazy pink condo apartment in a not-too-good part of town fetches in LA. They are so resented in their new home that a few vacationing Californians have taken to putting bumper stickers on their cars, saying: 'Don't Worry – Just Visiting'.

You can see why people go there. Seattle is gorgeous. It has more waterways than Venice, and more people there own boats than in any other American city. In good weather Mount Rainier, sixty miles away, seems to be floating just to one side, like Fuji.

The impact of the yuppies has been sudden and obvious. For instance, it is hard to find a rotten cup of coffee in Seattle. (American coffee is many times more reliable than British, but they do tend to serve it a little weak. The consequence is that, in order to absorb sufficient caffeine of a morning, it is necessary to drink half a gallon of a substance which has only marginally more taste than the average can of Budweiser beer, and even less stimulant effect.)

Seattle certainly appears to have more coffee bars per inhabitant than any other major city in the world. One of the many ignorant, racist charges made against yuppies is that they are only interested in stock options and high-definition television sets. It seems to me that they are much more concerned with what they put in their faces. In Seattle, if you are not near a coffee shop, then you are certainly near one of the new mobile coffee carts. It's astonishing that the citizenry doesn't go round permanently wired, bumping into each other, like Muppets with a thyroid problem.

Since they're going to ingest them, yuppies treat food and drink with a pedantic reverence. Once you reach the end of the long line at a popular coffee bar, like the successful Starbuck's chain, there's no way you can merely say, 'Gimme a coffee, black.' There's always some wispy-haired youth behind the counter who wants to introduce you to your beverage. 'This is a selected high mountain-grown bean from Colombia, which we roast ourselves, very lightly . . .' How can you consume something that has almost become a personal friend?

One of the most delicious drinks you can obtain in Seattle is iced latte. The wispy youth grinds up the beans for you, pops them into an espresso machine, and extracts from them perhaps one ounce of a thick, viscous fluid. Then he fills the glass with ice, tops it up with creamy milk, and at the last minute adds the vial of liquid engineering.

Seattle also has the nicest indoor market I've ever seen. It's huge and overlooks the magnificent waterfront. Developers wanted to knock it down, of course, but an alliance of locals and yuppies saved it, and now it's become a vast Victorian monument to the abundance of the region. The fish stalls are stacked high with crabs eighteen inches wide, silver banks of salmon in four or five varieties, three types of cod (to taste the cod smoked over alder wood is to get some idea of what table d'hôte must be like in Valhalla), pink prawns, black prawns, striped prawns, jumbo prawns, baby lobsters, crayfish, halibut, swordfish, mahi mahi, clams, oysters as big as turtles (well, nearly) for around 3 dollars a dozen, and the legs of Alaska king crabs, each so big they could break a swan's wing with a single blow.

Yuppies require that everything they eat is slightly different from that ingested by the commonality, so the market is filled with weird genetic experiments, as if the crops had been grown too near a leaky nuclear power station. You can find asparagus as thin as straw, elephant garlic as big as onions, tiny champagne grapes no larger than peas. There are beefsteak tomatoes which would make a whole meal, Italian plum tomatoes and tiny yellow 'teardrop' tomatoes. They sell punnets of blueberries, bilberries, blackberries, boysenberries, huckleberries, strawberries, and even yellow raspberries. You can hear the waiter now: 'Sir, we take fresh king salmon steaks, grill them over mesquite wood, and serve them with sweet basil, roasted elephant garlic, and a coulis of teardrop tomato and yellow raspberries . . .' 'Aargh,' you cry, 'in that case, bring me a cheeseburger!'

EAST ST LOUIS

East St Louis, Illinois, is the worst place in America. Oh, there may well be other claimants to the title. In America being the most of anything, even the most unspeakable, confers a measure of distinction. But it's hard to think of anywhere which could rival East St Louis for the consistency of its horrors.

The town can stand as a symbol for what are generally euphemized as America's 'inner cities', except that in East St Louis there are no pleasant leafy suburbs or bustling downtown shopping malls. There is inner city and nothing else. It may be the only municipality in America in which every single street is dangerous.

Like many hellish places, it is near some of the most agreeable. It's a ten-minute drive down Interstate 64 from Ladue, Missouri, a suburb of St Louis proper, and one of the half-dozen richest townships in the US. The *per capita* income there is ten times as high as in its neighbour. It has rolling lawns, perfectly tended churches, shopping malls filled with designer clothes stores. There are Volvos, BMWs, horses. None of these exists across the Mississippi in East St Louis.

It has become a kind of modern Gehenna. Physically it is right in the middle of America. In every other way, it might as well have dropped off the map.

The level of violence is so high that the Mayor's bodyguards carry Uzi sub-machine-guns. The city has no money at all; instead it has a debt of around 50 million dollars, which per head is slightly worse than Poland. Consequently, the sewer system broke down and could not be repaired. In 1989, the city was ordered by a court to clean up a two-acre lake of raw sewage which had flooded a housing development. Rubbish is almost never collected, and was once left to rot in the streets for more than a year. People tend to pile it on to the many vacant lots and burned-out houses, where it feeds the vermin who are so much more numerous than the human population.

The police – thought to be the most aged force in America – have half the numbers they would need in a town with an average crime rate. In East St Louis they are hopelessly outnumbered. At night, there are large parts of the city where they do not dare to go, even in pairs, heavily armed. For one thing, the drug dealers shoot the lights out. The Police Chief, Isadore Chambers, said, 'It would be suicide to send my men into the projects at night.'

City employees of all kinds, including firemen, often go for weeks unpaid. A third of the teachers had to be sacked recently because there was no money to pay them. People who work at the City Hall have to bring their own toilet paper to work because there is not enough money in the municipal coffers to supply it.

The population is declining too fast for anyone to be sure what it is, but estimates vary from 40,000 to 50,000 people, 98 per cent of whom are black, though this may be an underestimate. Certainly I was the only white person I saw during my visit. Two-thirds of the population are on welfare. The principal business is drug dealing.

Not long ago, a twelve-storey office block in what is laughably called 'the business district' was sold for 25,000 dollars, a sum which might get you an extra bathroom in Ladue. In summer the town looks almost lively, though this is largely because nobody has anywhere else to go but outside. Whole blocks of houses are derelict, boarded up or burnt out. A few wrecked shops and offices (only 200 businesses in the city still operate, after a fashion) have pathetic 'For Sale' notices in what were once their windows.

Anything that could be sold – bricks, gutterspouts, even man-hole covers – has been thieved. You can literally go for miles without seeing anything left worth stealing.

Hoboes pick through the piles of garbage. But what kind of garbage is left by people who have nothing in the first place? One low-rise project looked almost pleasant, with children shouting and playing on the grass. Then I saw the filthy stream of sewage oozing up from a crack in the sidewalk.

The week before I arrived, Police Chief Chambers brought his entire day shift together and sent them out to the big drug market at Broadway and 15th Street (the address, reminiscent of New

York, increases the sense of pathos). 'You should have seen them, forty, maybe fifty of them, running off when we showed up,' said the Chief, with a somewhat hollow laugh.

The best the police can do is move the pushers a block away; they prefer to stay near where their customers can find them. Since many buyers are white professionals from the pleasanter neighbourhoods across the river, they do not wish to pass time cruising around the streets. Nobody wants to spend longer in East St Louis than they must.

When I reached Broadway and 15th it seemed quiet enough, but I turned into 14th Street next, and was briefly stuck in a traffic jam, a short queue of motorists waiting to buy drugs. The dealers had the practised ease of staff at a drive-in burger joint. It was 3.30 in the afternoon.

In the distant mists of time, say back in the 1960s, East St Louis was a prosperous town, a railhead and stockyard second only to Chicago. Miles Davis, the jazz trumpeter, came from there. So did Ike Turner, Tina's ex-husband and first partner. She lived in the town too. So did Jackie Joyner Kersee, the Olympic gold medallist, who returns occasionally. But new transport systems and storage methods killed the stockyards. Other businesses folded with them. As unemployment and the crime rate rose, white flight to other suburbs left an ever-smaller tax base to cope with a spiralling proportion of poor. So city taxes were raised, which drove out more businesses and left the population even poorer. In two decades, the city's 'tax base', or rateable value, fell by 70 per cent.

Then in the 1980s the vicious circle was tightened by the arrival of 'crack', which is much cheaper than pure cocaine, much more powerful, and much more profitable. It makes its users violent and paranoid which is why the most common crime in East St Louis, apart from dealing in the stuff, is domestic assault.

The city could borrow money from the State of Illinois, but the Governor won't fork out unless the Mayor, one Carl Officer, resigns. Mayor Officer, one of the rare citizens who gets holidays, usually in Africa and at someone else's expense, also has an elegant funeral parlour, which is one of the few smart, clean buildings in the city, and does splendidly brisk business. In 1988 Officer was accused of improperly receiving 80,000 dollars in public funds. The charges were dropped when it turned out that the relevant records had been destroyed, 'in a fire'.

The following year the Reverend Joseph Davis, a close friend of the Mayor, was convicted of operating a big cocaine ring. Davis owned a Jaguar, also unusual in East St Louis, and was said to entice children into church by offering them cocaine.

There seems to be no way of solving the city's problems. There was a scheme to build luxury apartments on the river facing St Louis proper, whose yuppies would live there and pay taxes to East St Louis. But the company which came up with the scheme had to drop it after being accused of bribery elsewhere, and in any case the site was on a flood plain.

Yet life does go on. The young people's jazz band is usually voted best in the country, and the school athletes are among the best in the State, something which matters a great deal in the US, and particularly in the Midwest. But for many of the kids, there is no way out at all. The brightest cannot afford to go to college. So they can either get a job flipping hamburgers for 3.25 dollars an hour, or try to break into the drug trade, though this is risky. In a typical year, roughly one citizen in 600 is murdered, a *per capita* rate roughly twenty times that of Northern Ireland, and on a day-to-day basis worse than Beirut.

The unique horror of East St Louis is its isolation; it is unrelievedly awful in every particular. To misquote Gertrude Stein, the only 'there' there is there is appalling. South Chicago, East Los Angeles, Anacostia in Washington are all attached to big, mainly prosperous cities. Tax money is available. Essential services can be maintained, up to a point. A pretence of law and order can be offered.

It is a thin pretence. In Washington there was a heroin market a twenty-minute walk from the agreeable middle-class home which we rented. (The term 'street market' makes them sound like cheery barrow boys waving bunches of bananas. In fact it's a group of young men, maybe as many as thirty strong, hanging around. You can tell they are working because they look at the

58

street rather than at each other, and because, if it starts to rain, they produce ponchos and stay put.)

The police know precisely where every drug market is located, and exactly what the merchants there sell, for what price. They would love to scoop them up in the back of a van, but they can't. For one thing, the dealers rarely have the stuff on them. Instead they have 'runners' who collect it from stashes held by 'holders' some distance away.

No one ever says: 'Excuse me, I would like to buy some cocaine. Do you have any?' to receive the reply, 'Certainly, how much would you require?' The deal is conducted in an ambiguous code. 'Hey, my man, what's happening?' says the pusher, or some similarly vague street phrase. The customer might say, 'Gimme one.' This means a 10 dollar 'rock' of crack, but in a court transcript, they could appear to be trading in Hershey bars. As with chocolate, the dealers believe in brand loyalty, and the drugs actually have names. They will say, 'I got "Downtown"', or 'I got "Rambo".' The brand image is always macho and streetwise.

Of course the police use plain-clothes officers in unmarked cars, but after a while most of these are known. Small boys, known in Washington as 'pee wees', are paid 50 dollars a night to watch out for the police. Somewhat older boys, some still at school, are dealers in their own right. This work so interfered with classes that many schools have banned the beepers which customers used to summon them.

Naturally the dealers all monitor closely the police radio network. The police tried to photocopy the money they were using for big deals, then use it as evidence after they'd arrested people. It took the pushers all of twenty-four hours to work that one out, and the money was resting in the cash registers of the kind of store which sells chunky gold jewellery before the cops arrived to claim it back.

Arrests don't end the problem. As soon as someone is removed, someone else arrives on the same corner to take his place. The process of the law is slow; defence attorneys are well paid and effective. The profits are high and the risk seems acceptable. Sell drugs and you wear designer clothes and drive an expensive

German car. Of course you run the risk of arrest, and the somewhat lesser risk of a spell in jail. Sell hamburgers or clean streets and you are nothing, perhaps for the rest of your life.

This will continue indefinitely because the whole drug culture is entirely demand-led. The customers are not only the black underclass; the police pick up lawyers, doctors, congressional aides, lots of middle-class people from the suburbs. In some circles, hard liquor is more frowned upon than cocaine. It is grotesque that the administration tries to bully impoverished Latin American countries to stop growing the vegetation which supplies the drugs. Grotesque and pointless. As long as a Colombian peasant can earn 1,000 dollars a year growing coca instead of 90 dollars growing coffee, he will. Why should he not? America's drug problem is entirely due to America's drug users.

As long as this remains the case, there seems little hope. One could conceive of some ruthless tyrant taking action, as if a Saddam Hussein were to become President and decide to send the army in to mow down the pushers with machine guns, together with whichever of their clients happened to be there at the time. The dealers would simply fire back. They are adequately armed, chiefly with Uzis and AK-47s. The army might not even win, because the pushers would be fighting on their own turf.

Another method would be to destroy the streets where they lived. Mayor Wilson Goode of Philadelphia tried exactly that with an uppity group of citizens in 1965, bombing several ghetto blocks from the air. He did subsequently win re-election, but even in Philadelphia it was not thought necessarily practical to launch a blitzkrieg against your own city.

TWO

Talking Heads

George Bernard Shaw may have said that 'England and America are two countries separated by the same language', though since the quote appears in none of his published writings, and cropped up for the first time in a 1942 edition of the *Reader's Digest*, it seems fairly likely that he didn't.

In any event, he would have been wrong. Modern British English is a dialect of the principal tongue, American English. Quite a close dialect, too. An educated Londoner would have no problem understanding 95 per cent of what was said by an educated citizen of, say, Chicago – though he might have great trouble with his own countrymen in northern Scotland or even some parts of London.

Our shared tongue does allow for some confusion, though it usually comes where you least expect it. By now everyone knows that an elevator is a lift, that a diaper is a nappy, that a tap is a faucet (though Americans use 'tap water'), and a toilet is a bathroom (though they do use 'toilet paper'). But 'pavement' is sometimes puzzling, since in American English it means the paved part of the road, and so is sometimes used in the exact opposite sense to 'sidewalk', to the bewilderment of British drivers already trying to cope with automatic transmission and automatic seatbelts, which clamp you to the car, as if in some high-tech torture chamber.

Friends were startled to hear, on the day we moved to a new flat, that the 'removal men' had been round. Your furniture is shifted by 'movers'; 'removal men' generally work for undertakers. We baffled folk by inviting them round for Sunday lunch and promising a 'joint'. A leg of lamb or a slab of beef is a 'roast', a 'joint' is quite different. There are other unexpected traps. I miffed a friend who was wearing a new suit by saying that he looked particularly 'smart'. The word only means 'intelligent' in the US, so I had implied that he usually looked comparatively stupid.

'Cheap' is almost exclusively pejorative in America and means either 'second-rate' or, of a person, someone who is too tight-fisted to buy anything better. A host who offered a 'cheap' bottle of wine in Britain might be praised for his skill at ferreting out a bargain; in the US he would just be a lousy host. On the other hand, in American English, the term 'mean' has nothing to do with money. A 'mean' person is ill-natured; someone who won't spend his money is, well, 'cheap'.

In English English the modifier 'quite' has two different, contradictory meanings. 'Quite nice' would mean merely mediocre, while 'quite superb' is the opposite. But there's no ambiguity in American usage. An English friend was sorry to be told by an American that an article he'd written was 'quite good', until he learned that this meant 'first-rate'.

Most Americans in Britain already know that a dirty word such as 'fags' means cigarettes (a delicacy on sale in North of England grocery stores, known as 'Brain's Frozen Faggots', used to render some visitors helpless with laughter). They know that 'knocking up' means nothing more than persuading voters to the polls – though one female British MP caused nationwide delight in the US when she described her election day: 'I start by knocking up . . . after lunch I go knocking up again, and I keep knocking up until the polls close.'

Americans in Britain were delighted a few years ago to see billboards everywhere bearing the slogan: 'Nothing Sucks Like An Electrolux'. To say that something 'sucks' is to use America's most common term of disparagement. On the whole, American slang moves from the filthy to the genteel. The term 'suck' in this context originally had as its prefix the word for a male hen which the Puritans changed, for decency's sake, to 'rooster', since it has had numerous meanings, some obscene, for centuries. But nowadays 'suck' is used by almost everyone. Small children can say it without risking reproof.

'Nuts', an expletive now so mild that a nun could use it, originally had only a metaphorical relationship to arboreal seed casings. 'Mother' abbreviates a longer phrase which meant 'one who commits incest'; now, 'Let's get this mother on the road' is perfectly acceptable and one day might be used by bishops.

On the whole, I think, British slang is richer than American, partly because we absorb theirs while inventing our own. They see almost exclusively American TV and American films, so are dipping into a smaller pool. (Australia has a particularly rich stock of slang, since they see their own, British and American TV.) Once, for a curious American friend, I tried to write down all the slang terms for sexual intercourse which would be understood in modern Britain. I ran out at forty-three. He still gets it wrong, and sounds like a tourist who has learned only from a Berlitz course. 'Am I correct in calling this a "bonking" good meal?' he will ask.

According to William Safire, America's leading lexicographical journalist, more English English is entering the US, possibly as a result of British television, which is seen by a small but articulate minority of people through the Public Broadcasting System. Indeed, Sunday night on many PBS stations is almost thrown over to British TV: inferior costume dramas, repeats of *Monty Python* and sitcoms starring Penelope Keith, for the most part. In these, people insist on saying 'fridge' instead of 'icebox' or 'refrigerator', 'pricey' instead of 'expensive', 'early on', 'smarmy', 'trendy' and several other words which are slowly infiltrating American English, even though the main flow is, as ever, in the opposite direction.

Cinema snobs in America talk about 'films', instead of 'movies', whereas the opposite is true in Britain. Their use of 'film' implies a sense of cinema as art; ours brags of a familiarity with Hollywood terminology. America kept some older forms of English; the example usually cited is 'gotten' as the past participle of 'got', though this too is becoming rarer, perhaps as a result of general slovenliness. But some of the phrases they have kept must cause puzzlement. 'In for a penny, in for a pound' is fairly commonly used, though whereas a 'penny' is a one-cent coin, a 'pound' is only a unit of weight. (America has rightly insisted on

63

rejecting the metric system for everything except scientific and industrial purposes. Nobody talks about metres or litres or grams. Very occasionally you will see a road sign giving kilometres as well as miles, but this has usually been placed by some federal agency on a tourist route. What the US has realized is, that while it may be necessary to deal in millimetres and the like when you are selling precision machine tools to the Germans or Taiwanese, it makes no difference at all to anyone how you sell your milk, measure a football pitch or judge the distance from Dallas to Fort Worth.)

Americans may have less slang, but it is particularly vigorous. Much of it is macho, designed to reveal the user as tough and clear-eyed about the true state of the world. Businessmen's talk, for instance, has a swaggering, no nonsense, 'I'm-on-top-of-this' quality. The concept of 'the bottom line' means 'What's in it for me? Don't waste my time with irrelevancies.' No rival business merely heads for failure, but is 'a basket case'. Close competition is 'going to the wire', a racing metaphor which evokes the thunder of hooves for what may merely be a marginal difference in a tender.

Even the mildest office worker will sometimes try to describe his work in ferocious locker-room terminology. 'I've been kicking some ass round here today', probably means 'I wrote two stiffly worded memos.' 'Lissen, pal, I wrestled him to the mat' can be translated as 'We disagreed on the issue, but I think I managed to convey my point of view.'

During the run-up to the 1988 presidential election I went to see a Dukakis fund-raiser, who was confident that his candidate would win the Democratic nomination over his then chief rival, Gary Hart. 'We'll clean his clock,' he said, mystifyingly. Next day I lunched with an aide to Hart, who dismissed the Dukakis challenge. 'We'll clean his clock!' he announced. I am told the term comes from boxing.

Sport is full of beefy phrases, especially from baseball, which has been played professionally for longer than the others. Assistants to a politician who has made a successful speech will claim that 'he hit it out of the park'. If someone is 'home safe', they've

64

won a close, touch-and-go decision. 'Getting to first base' is a universal term for beginning an enterprise with a degree of success, whether it's persuading a client to consider an offer or getting a kiss on a first date. A 'curveball' is any difficult challenge, such as a hard-to-answer question. All these expressions are used in an appropriate fashion, though they have the added advantage of bringing a hard, masculine flavour to the conversation. 'That came out of left field' has an edge which the mere 'That was unexpected' lacks.

(The power of baseball terminology has been recognized by the Quebecois, who support the only Francophone baseball team, the Montreal Expos. At least the fans are Francophone; the players, like so many others in the major leagues, tend to come from Cuba and Dominica. The authorities had someone translate all baseball words into French for the purposes of broadcasting commentaries, so a batter is a *'frappeur'*, a pitcher *'un lanceur'*, and so forth. They even saw the need to translate the slang, so that, for example, the base is *'le sac'*, an exact translation of the American 'bag'.)

There are other curiosities of American speech which reveal themselves more slowly. Often phrases which are designed to intensify say the opposite of what the speaker means. I'm not referring here to 'Let's do lunch', which can mean 'I hope I never see you again', but, for instance, to 'I could care less', which means 'I *couldn't* care less'. The best-known example is 'You don't say', which means, 'Repeat to me what you just said because I find it hard to believe'. 'Tell me about it' means 'Don't tell me about it', as in, 'The traffic was terrible on the freeway.' 'Tell me about it.'

Americans often use the qualifier which precedes a noun to stand for the noun itself. Nobody ever eats a 'Danish pastry' any more, only a 'Danish'. 'Shocks' are shock absorbers. I saw a sign in New York advertising 'Wallets – 24 for $6.99', which seemed good value, until I realized that it meant 'wallet-sized photos'.

'Guy' is a strange case. It used to mean specifically male persons, as in *Guys and Dolls*. Now it is unisex, and may even be used more often by women of women. It's not unusual to see a mother address her daughter and girlfriends as 'guys'.

Teenage slang changes fairly fast, but not as quickly as you might imagine. Much of it began in California, but was spread around the country, and so fossilized as a kind of nationally approved teen-speak by popular films such as *Fast Times at Ridgemount High* and *Teenage Mutant Ninja Turtles*. 'Awesome', 'radical', 'cool' and 'excellent' (sometimes intensified to 'indubitably excellent') are terms of praise. A good-looking girl is a 'fox'. The universal black term 'dudes' for 'male persons' sometimes becomes 'dudettes' for females.

American teenagers have learned how to dispense with the verb 'to say', and it's possible to hear long reports of conversations in which the word is never used. 'So I'm like, "Where were you?" and he's like, "Why do you care?"' But then Americans are skilled at non-verbal communication. 'Uh-oh' (with the voice falling) means 'oh dear', and was the last utterance of the *Challenger* captain before the shuttle exploded. 'Uh-huh' (voice rising) means either 'yes', or 'you're welcome', a phrase which puzzlingly appears sometimes in the form 'you bet'. Thank you for your help.' 'You bet.' 'Uh-uh' (voice falling slightly) means 'no'. 'Uh-ohhh' (voice on the same level, but lengthened on the second beat) means 'watch out, be careful', as to a child about to spill something. Other noises, depending on the tone in which they are hummed, can mean 'probably', 'probably not' or even 'that would be wonderful!'

By the same token, Americans think the British are masters of the baffling grunt. We use the sound 'mmm' to convey a range of meanings, from 'yes', 'without doubt', through 'I don't think so', to 'I am not really paying attention but I suppose what you just said is all right'.

There are strange regional usages. Once, covering a serious drought in the Midwest, I called on a farmers' representative in North Dakota and asked him to put me in touch with a family who would help. He phoned a couple and wanted to assure them that I was an amiable fellow. 'I know you'll enjoy visiting with him,' he said. I tried say that I didn't want *them* to visit me; I would rather go to their farm. He couldn't understand my confusion; there 'visit with' merely means 'talk to'. In the same region people say politely, 'Thank you much.'

There is a 'y'all' line across America, roughly coinciding with the Mason-Dixon Line which divides the South from the North along the Pennsylvania-Maryland border. 'Y'all' does not refer to a group of people, but is simply the plural of 'you', and corresponds to the Irish 'youse'. A couple having a meal south of the y'all line will be asked at the end, 'Y'all having coffee?' or 'Y'all enjoy your meal?'

In the South an elaborate but sometimes empty form of verbal courtesy is often thought essential for all social occasions. Once I stayed in a motel in Arlington, Texas, where the staff were surprisingly rude and off-hand. (This was unusual. They might be inefficient, but in the South a somewhat over-the-top courtesy is thought *de rigueur*, at least for dealing with white people.) As I gratefully left, the cashier said something which sounded like, 'Yurry-bah-seas-yurr?' It was only when I'd made it to the car-park that I realized she'd been trying to say, 'You hurry back and see us, you hear?' It was the contrast between the meaning of the message and the surly tone in which it was delivered which was so disjointing – and startling in such a courteous part of a courteous nation.

But accents were always a problem. Once I was on the terrifying 'Space Mountain' roller-coaster at Disneyland, in California. An English couple, fairly upper-class, were sitting behind me. The disembodied electronic voice declared: 'Prepare to Launch! Prepare to Launch!'

The woman turned to her husband and inquired, 'Lunch? Lunch? Do they really serve lunch on this thing?'

THREE

The Way They Live Now

Medieval schoolmen used to argue over whether Hell could be defined as the experience of absolute cold alternating with equally terrible heat. Among the factors they had to consider was this: since there would be a fraction of a second of bliss as you moved from one intolerable temperature to its equally intolerable opposite, could it be truly described as Hell?

As if to answer the question, the modern American home has come to the same arrangement. During summer in say, the Midwest, the temperature outside may be 100°F, and the relative humidity 100 per cent. But inside it is freezing, like a meat store. In winter, the temperature can be 30° below zero, but indoors it's up to 80°. Imagine wrapping yourself in a duvet and a fur coat – then stepping into a sauna. The moment of bliss is fleeting at best.

The general idea is that a home is at the right temperature if, while indoors, you can wear clothes which are the exact opposite of those appropriate for the season. If it's freezing outside, you should be able to wear a T-shirt and shorts in the house. If it's sweltering outside and you can actually watch the grass turning brown on the lawn, then you should be comfortable in a thick woollen sweater.

This is why Jimmy Carter caused himself such trouble one winter when he suggested that everyone turn the thermostat in their homes down to 65° in order to save energy. In fact, 65 is a perfectly pleasant temperature, and if you're chilly, then you could wear an undershirt or something sensible in wool. But this is not how Americans tend to think. To make matters worse, Carter (already perceived as a pious prig) addressed the nation wearing a beige cardigan, a garment which had a dreary worthiness embedded in every fibre. But even if it had been a shimmering Yves St Laurent sweater made of a lustrous sleek mohair, the principle would have been wrong. Americans have a God-given right not to wear sweaters in the house if they don't want to, even in the dead of winter. Carter might as well have told them that, in order to preserve vital fruit supplies, they should not eat apple pie.

I can understand this belief in contra-climactic conditioning in shops and bars and places of entertainment. People don't want to spend their money in establishments which are tight-fisted with fuel. 'Come on in, it's c-o-o-o-l inside' was a popular sign outside cinemas in summer, and, unlike Europe, summer is the busiest period for the movie industry. The cold is one of the main attractions, so much so that people actually take sweaters along with them to the movies, especially when the temperature outside is in the 90s. Apart from the fact that you would otherwise sit in your seat with your teeth chattering, imagine the horror of emerging into the Turkish bath outdoors and having nothing to take off.

In winter, department stores sometimes arrange for a curtain of air so hot you can see it blast from above the front door down to street level. Go from the cold outside across this curtain once or twice, and you can recreate exactly how a doner kebab feels on a spit. Inside the store it's fractionally more temperate, but the message is the same: 'We're not mean, look, we'll keep you warmer than you could ever need!' In the more upmarket stores it's possible to see women in fur coats wandering around the racks, surreptitiously mopping their faces to keep the sweat from glistening. You can lose as much weight buying a new shower curtain as you would in a forty-five-minute Jane Fonda workout.

This obsession with inverting the temperature tells us, I think, something about the United States. I suspect it's connected to the basic American dread that there might not be enough. America is a huge country, but in more than just acreage: so much inside it is vast as well. It has to be; otherwise you would have this fear that it might not be enough, that you might run out. For the

people who came to this abundant continent, and their descend-
ants today, it was not enough to have escaped poverty and hunger;
they had to put as great a distance between it and them as they
possibly could. Of course there are many poor people in the United
States, and they are visible on every corner in the centre of most
big cities. But they, too, share the American dream: one day they
will have more – far more – than enough of everything, including
food and heat. Somewhere behind the mournful cry 'godany-
change?' stands the Big Rock Candy Mountain.

(Beggars tend to stick together for company and comfort, with
the result that you might be approached ten times in a hundred
yards. Once after giving away my last quarter in downtown Washington, I yelled at the final panhandler: 'No, I haven't got any
more, dammit!' He beamed and said, 'Well, have a nice day
anyway, sir.' Naturally I gave him seventy-five cents the next
time I passed him. One beggar in New York wanted money 'to
return to my own planet. Gimme a dollar and I'll take Reagan.
But I'm not taking Bush.')

Fridges in American homes are the size of wardrobes, and have
to be, to accommodate the gallon bottles of milk and the 5 lb.
tubs of butter. Wardrobes (known as 'walk-in closets') are the size
of small rooms. Everybody knows about the restaurants where
they sell you steaks which are too big to fit on the plate, but the
sweet smell of excess permeates everywhere. 7-Eleven stores sell
a soft drink known as 'The Big Gulp', 32 fluid ounces or two
American pints of ice and fizzy water. Drink one of those on a
hot day, and you sound like Vesuvius the day before Pompeii
copped it.

Newspapers are so big and fat that you can get a hernia picking
them up from the doorstep. Magazine articles aren't for skimming
over a cup of coffee; they have lasting value, long-lasting value.
You could take a single copy of the *New Yorker* on a trek to the
North Pole and still have plenty left over to read when you got
home again. They once carried a series of three articles, each more
than 20,000 words long, on the uses of asbestos in American
industry. That is more information about the use of asbestos in
industry than anyone could need to know, including an expert on

industrial uses for asbestos. In America you are not allowed to run out of *anything*.

Roseanne Barr used to have a routine in which she imagined Louis XVI coming to visit her trailer home. *'Mon Dieu,'* he said, 'ziss is even more magnifique than mah palace at Versailles!' Naturally few American homes resemble Versailles, though they do exist. The point is, though, that it's something to aim for.

In Britain even the middle classes favour a discreet shabbiness in the décor. We have a range of phrases to express disapproval of anywhere that is too clean, too neat, too smartly polished: 'It looks unlived in,' we say, 'they must chain the kids up to keep it looking that way.' This does not apply in the United States. Your home is an extension of yourself, and you would no more have it looking less than perfect when guests came round than you would go to an important meeting with an egg stain on your tie. A friend reported a chilling conversation he'd had in California. He had asked how a mutual acquaintance was doing. 'Not too good,' he was told. How did they know? 'I've been to his home,' was the answer. The assumption was that the man's financial good standing would have been instantly reflected in his house.

Our home in Washington struck English visitors as fairly grand, but probably had less effect on Americans, who were, of course, too polite to pass comment. There were scratches on the floor where we had moved heavy furniture. Perilous piles of magazines swayed next to the telephone. We were fond of a particularly comfortable armchair which we kept in the living-room, in spite of the fact that the stuffing was coming out of one arm. It would have cost hundreds to re-upholster, and since it had cost only 25 dollars, there seemed no point. It's the kind of item that would have looked entirely right in a stately home (at least the part the impoverished earl lives in, not the bit that's open to the public). But most of our American friends were probably as surprised to see it sitting there as they would have been if the dining-room table had been propped up by old phone directories. But then it was a very English type of room.

Americans are tremendously polite. The world tends to believe

71

that they aren't. According to some movies, when an American meets another American, one of two things is likely to happen.

Either (1) the greeter cries: 'H'are yah, my ol' buddy, my ol' frien', yew no good son-of-a-gun, yew!' while slapping him heartily on the back.

Or (2) he kills him.

Naturally the second is more frequent than the first, especially in some of the rougher parts of the country. On the other hand, neither is common. Most Americans, on meeting, treat each other in a fashion which would please the director of protocol at a Japanese royal funeral.

Suppose you see an old friend in the street. He is talking to two people you don't know. You wave to him in greeting. A conversation along these lines next takes place:

Your friend: Simon, it's good to see you. I'd like to have you meet Al and Frank.

Al: It's good to meet you, Simon.

You: It's good to meet you too, Al.

Frank: I'm pleased to meet you, Simon.

You: And I'm delighted to meet you as well, Frank.

Your friend: How is your wife, Simon?

You: Well, it's funny you should ask. Right now our house is on fire, and she's trapped on the top floor with the children. Not surprisingly, our phone is down, so I'm on my way to call the Fire Department from a neighbour's house. I hope they don't take too long!

Your friend: Well, in that case, I guess we shouldn't keep you! I sure hope you find a phone!

Al: Me too. It's been good to meet you, Simon.

And so forth, and so on. At the end of this exchange you have also shaken hands six times, once with each person on arrival and departure. Visiting foreigners, under the impression that Americans are 'casual', quickly make mistakes. For instance, at any social gathering, it is essential to say goodbye to each departing guest, adding some indication that having made their acquaintance was the most fascinating social experience you have had since you were last kidnapped by space bimbos from the Planet

Zaargh, even if you did not actually address a single word to them, or they to you, throughout the whole event.

Next time you meet them you can repeat the entire ritual. 'I do believe I had the pleasure of meeting you at the Richardsons,' you say. 'Why, so we did. It's so good to meet you again' – possibly the last words you will hear from them until it's time to say goodbye and run through the whole performance again. In polite American society, parting is neither sweet nor sorrowful, just very time consuming.

Americans *are* informal, but their rules of informal etiquette are just as demanding as those which apply among the diplomatic corps. In Britain we tend to imagine that informal means 'off-hand'. In the US, it's the opposite. There's an intensity to their informality. If you run into someone by chance, the phrase, 'Well, hi, how *are* you?' has to be said with an emphasis which implies that your meeting is the most delightful circumstance since Dante first whistled at Beatrice. Whereas most English people would hop from one foot to the other while trying to work up something to say, an American will announce that he has a plan, which is to go down to a certain watering hole he knows where you and he are going to down a few beers . . . British people imagine that the invitation is so specific that it would be offensive to refuse. But it isn't. The invitation must be specific, because otherwise it wouldn't sound real: 'Why don't we have a drink some time?' really would be off-hand, even rude, in American terms.

When Americans meet abroad, or even in America, if they are strangers there is a ritual they must go through, which is a crucial part of their code of behaviour. It might be called the Geographical Link and it is the American equivalent of the handshake, the essential form of introduction.

Party A: Now, where are you folks from?

Party B: We're from Dayton, Ohio.

A: Well, is that so? You know my husband Everett had a cousin – a second cousin, that is – who used to live in Cincinatti, Ohio.

B: Well, hey, I was in Cincinatti only a couple months back!

A: You were? Now I wish I could remember my cousin's name

. . . of course, I think he moved to Anchorage, or maybe it was Miami?

Not that this matters, because the Geographical Link is established and courtesy has been observed. My wife and I once went on a tour of China in a party which included six Americans, who between them came from four different places. Most of our first dinner together consisted on finding the Link between all these different pairs. Anything will do: 'My help once told me she had family in Tulsa' is quite adequate.

People laugh at American courtesy and assume that it indicates insincerity. They mock phrases like 'Have a nice day' and ask whether anyone who utters it cares at all what the next twenty-four hours hold for the recipient.

Of course they don't, but then no one who asks 'How are you?' wants or expects a run-down on the addressee's medical condition. 'Have a nice day' is a form of words which is as necessary to smooth social functioning as the tortured phrases such as '*Veuillez assurez-vous, cher monsieur, l'expression . . .*' which French people put at the end of their letters. I once tried to hire a car in Maine and got a recorded message: 'Thank you for calling Hertz Rent-a-Car. I'm sorry, we have no cars now. Have a nice day!'

So inbuilt are these social graces that many people find it impossible to break them, even under severe pressure. In Washington, I once stood waiting to buy a plane ticket behind a woman who tried to pay first by cheque, then with an outdated credit card. She was exceedingly grand, and the counter clerk was surly (there was a racial sub-text, too; the clerk was poor white, the customer well-to-do black).

In the end, after some twenty minutes of ill-feeling, the customer admitted defeat. As she stalked off she turned round, ready to utter some crushing phrase which would leave the clerk with as much dignity as a used wet-wipe. But she couldn't. Years of conditioning prevented her. In the end, she flung over her shoulder this devastating put-down: 'Have a so-so day!'

The courtesy can be quite startling. Take smoking. It is now generally recognized throughout the United States that people who smoke in public are little better than serial killers, and should be treated that way, or at least be forced to go somewhere else to commit their slaughter.

Smokers who visit other people's houses expect to go through a humiliating little ritual. 'Could we ask you a really big favour?' they ask. 'You're welcome to say no.'

'You'd like to smoke? Why, you're most welcome,' we'd reply, fetching ashtrays and matches.

'But are you really sure?' they'd plead wonderingly.

'Of course,' we'd insist, offering a selection of cigar cutters, corn cob pipes, churchwardens, hubble-bubbles and tins of Red Man brand chewing tobacco, together with a silver spittoon. Even so, they would seem piteously grateful that we hadn't tossed them out of the house.

One freezing Christmas Eve we had two couples round for dinner. We were about to eat when we discovered that the two husbands were missing. We found them, like twin Captain Oateses, having a smoke outside, the butts tamped down by their chattering teeth.

Once I was at an American party where a somewhat boorish fellow-countryman of mine – a sort of Ugly Englishman – lit up a large cigar after the buffet dinner. 'How does he dare to do that?' asked my hostess in the way one might ask: 'Why do you English still thrash your children?' She suggested that I should remonstrate with him, as one Brit to another. I explained that it was for exactly this reason that I couldn't, so settled for a typical English compromise: as I walked past him, I coughed, loudly.

Of course it didn't work, because he wasn't culturally attuned. If I'd done the same to an American he would have looked like a departing guest from whose coat pockets a cascade of fish knives has just fallen.

The rules of informal etiquette as observed in the US state (or would state, if anyone had written them down) that it is rude to be too polite. An example. Once I was staying with friends of friends in a suburb of New York City. The weather outside was stiflingly hot, and we had just been playing badminton in the garden. The Arctic blast of air-conditioning was welcome, but I was still thirsty, so asked if I could have a beer from the fridge.

A look of near panic came over my host's face, a look which could be translated as, 'My God, we've got one of these Brits who is so goddam polite he's going to be knocking on our bedroom door at four a.m. to ask if he can take a leak, fer Chrissake.'

Of course, being American, he couldn't say anything remotely like that. Instead he gave me a courteous little lecture about how everything in his home was mine, and implied that if the mood took me, I should take bottles of vintage wines from his cellar, rare original oils from his wall, and pleasure his wife if I felt like it. All without asking.

I worked in Northern Ireland at the time, and while in Manhattan, had picked up a copy of the local Irish expatriates' newspaper. On returning to the house, I discovered that my hostess had kindly bought the same paper for me. I thanked her for her consideration, and put it aside. Later that evening she approached me with quivering jaw.

'Simon,' she said, 'I don't think you have read your Irish newspaper yet.'

'Er, no, I haven't. But I'm certainly looking forward to it.'

'Are you? Or is there something you haven't told me?'

The whole shaming story emerged: how I had pretended not to have seen the paper, how I had been so ill-at-ease in their home that I had not felt able to tell them frankly that I had already bought the paper, how hurt they were by my lack of candour, how much they had hoped I felt they were my friends.

And so on. An exaggerated response, certainly, but one which lies at the bottom of many American attitudes. If people expect to take you to their bosom the minute they meet you, then you have to respond by baring your own soul smartish as well.

For a Briton there is only one response to this charge of showing undue unfamiliarity, short of running screaming from the room, and that is to lapse into a kind of doddering, chinless, dear me, I'm afraid we British, gosh-you-must-think-we're-frighfully-buttoned-up-compared-to-you act, loosely based on old performances by Robert Morley and Wilfred Hyde-White. It is impossible to overstate the harm caused to Anglo-American relations by the recent rise of tough-guy British film stars such as

Michael Caine, Sean Connery and Edward Woodward, for whom, as the eponymous *Equaliser*, the stiff upper lip belonged to whomever he had last punched in the mouth. They are destroying that valuable silly-ass stereotype, leaving the rest of us with nowhere to hide.

Fortunately most Americans still tend to assume that we are terribly polite and that if a British person does it, then it must conform to some rule of etiquette, on the same grounds that if an Italian says something in Italian, he must be correct, even if it's actually gibberish. This belief even survives visits to, say, London, which is one of the rudest cities in the world, and I include New York. Time and again, I've read articles praising, for example, the courtesy of the London bus queue: 'Passengers still stand in line and climb aboard the bus in strict order of who came first,' they rave, regardless of the fact that no queue has been seen waiting for a London bus since approximately the time they stopped using horses to pull them.

Another element of American courtesy which can confuse visitors is the way you have to give a little gift of intimacy, rather like the bunch of flowers or chocolates which people take to dinner parties. I recall one woman friend describing at length the horrors which attended the birth of her first child, which wouldn't have been too bad, except for the fact that at the time we were enjoying a plate of ribs in barbecue sauce. I realized that this wasn't meant to spoil the meal, but was her present, a part of herself, an emotional keepsake. This is why Americans get upset if you don't confide the scoop about how your last love affair ended, or your emotions while standing over your mother's coffin, or how you felt when you suddenly thought that you might be impotent.

Not replying to your friend's story, about how she told the children she was going to get divorced, with a similarly gut-wrenching story about how you felt when you discovered your brother was a crack dealer is as rude in its way as failing to buy your round in a British pub.

One of the myths about American children is that they are spoiled brats. I have rarely found it so. Of course such children exist, but on the whole they are more polite and courteous than those in Britain. This may reflect partly on the parents, who sometimes appear to regard their children as a means of extending their own prestige and social standing.

Parents could be ferocious. Meeting children for the first time, I would try to persuade their parents that I did not require nor wish to be addressed as 'Mr Hoggart'. 'Simon' would do quite well. In this I almost invariably failed, since to relax the rule for some passing visitor would mean abandoning it altogether.

A scene like this was always possible:

Self: Whoops!

Hostess: What is it, Simon? Has Joey done something?

Self: Oh no, no, just a tiny spot of spaghetti sauce landed on my jeans. A complete accident, and it's no problem at all. Why, you can hardly see it!

Hostess: Joey, I think you owe Mr Hoggart an apology.

Joey (looks resentful)

Hostess (quietly): Joey, you will apologize to Mr Hoggart.

Self: Please, it really doesn't matter at all, really, I promise, no harm done.

Hostess: Simon, please leave this to me. JOEY YOU WILL APOLOGIZE TO MR HOGGART OR GO TO YOUR ROOM THIS INSTANT DO YOU HEAR ME?

(Child departs upstairs, sound of tantrum, breaking toys, TV on maximum volume.)

Hostess: I am so sorry. Now, Joey will be working every night when he gets back from school, mowing the neighbours' lawns, sitting their dogs and cleaning their chimneys, so he can earn the money to replace your jeans. He *has* to learn.

Of course next time you return to the house, Joey loathes your guts, and who can blame him? He'll be a drug abuser in ten years, if he isn't already.

American parents work awfully hard. It's a good rule of thumb that the more expensive a school is, the more work the parents have to do. There are soccer practice, school trips, fund-raising fairs, sometimes known as 'fayres'; in some schools they have a duty parent system. It costs a fortune, too. On top of the fees, which at the best schools can easily be 8,000 or 9,000 dollars a year, you are constantly having to dig into your trousers for more. Schools hold auctions, at which gifts given by the parents are sold off. They are worth having. A holiday, given by a travel agent. A porcelain dinner service, given by the local department store. A gourmet dinner for twelve, cooked in your own home.

At a fancy school like Sidwell, in Washington (very few white people send their children to the free, state school; the best in town is Wilson High, where an argument about who sat next to which girl in the cafeteria ended in gunfire, wounding four pupils) the gifts donated are astounding: 5,000 dollars' worth of fine wine, a mink coat, a Persian rug, a week in the Virgin Islands on a fifty-foot yacht.

In Washington, the principal trading commodity is status. Newspaper columnists and TV reporters offer lunch – with themselves. One celebrated media couple gives a dinner with famous politicians, who talk to the lucky purchasers almost as equals; imagine how embarrassing that must be. Senator Bill Bradley, who used to be a basketball star, will shoot hoops with you and four friends. One year someone paid 2,000 dollars for that and thought he'd got a bargain. The humorist Art Buchwald will mention the lucky bidder as a 'fictional character' in one of his columns. Can't you see it now, framed and hanging in the toilet?

Americans are more snobbish than we, or they, generally think. They're just snobbish about different things. Other States, for example. I remember excitedly telling a friend in Washington, a senior civil servant, that we were about to go to California. He said in a stiff fashion, 'I have never been to California', as he might have said, 'I have never employed a male stripper.'

We asked why. 'Because,' he said grandly, 'if I had the time and money to go to California, I could go to London or Paris instead.'

I recall another friend getting extremely angry when someone, also British, praised the Midwest and its decent, hardworking people. They might be industrious, he conceded, but they were everything that was wrong about the United States: narrow, conservative, chauvinist in the old sense, the kind of people who voted for Ronald Reagan and thought that Dan Quayle really

79

did represent true American values. The conversation got quite heated; it was clear that part of his own self-esteem was tied up in not being from the Midwest.

There are cross-currents of regional snobbery which only reveal themselves slowly. New Yorkers regard California as a fictional place, a permanent studio set. Los Angeles they call dismissively 'La La Land'. Meanwhile the inhabitants of La La Land regard anyone who chooses not to live there as a throwback to an earlier, less civilized age. One January I was driving along a Los Angeles freeway listening to the radio. Outside the temperature was around 60°F and the palm trees were waving gently under the brown sky. The disc jockey was talking to a man in Redwing, Minnesota, which had been logged the previous day as the coldest place in the United States. The man was explaining that he couldn't go to work because an icicle had fallen off a truck and broken his windshield. The disc jockey was exultant as he described the weather in Los Angeles.

'Why doncha put all the population of Redwing into buses and come and live here?' he asked.

'Well, we wouldn't want to do that,' said the man in his slow Midwestern accent, 'we heard California is full of weirdos.'

North-easterners look down on Southerners, who claim to look down on them, but know that in a battle of snobbery there cannot be two winners, so tend to adopt an exaggerated Southern manner as a form of self-defence.

Virginians look down on West Virginians. People in New Hampshire, which is very prosperous, look down on Maine, which isn't and where one of the most favoured sports is 'pulling' a weighted flatbed with a powerful pick-up truck, through mud. Almost everyone looks down on 'Okies'. Coloradans look down on Texans ('If God had meant Texans to ski, he'd have made bullshit white'), though Texans cannot conceive that anyone might look down on them since they know that they come from, without any question, the finest State of them all. You can see them at Dallas or Houston airport, wearing their ten-gallon hats, boots and rhinestone-studded shirts, looking relaxed, confident and *big*. See them getting off the plane in New York or

Washington, and they just look silly, as silly as they would if they turned up wearing a 'Kiss Me, I'm Irish' badge at the Russian Tea Rooms in Manhattan.

People sometimes ask if Americans have a sense of humour. Of course they do; it's just different from ours. Americans do not regard life as a joke. They take it far more seriously than the British do, which is one reason why they are such a successful nation. Newspapers, for instance: they have their comic strips – spread over three pages in the *Washington Post*, for example – and there will be a humorous column, clearly so marked. But the notion of a witty and ironic news story is unimaginable, like a funny funeral. The news is sacrosanct, and there is no recognition that some matters are best understood through humour. The jokes have to be set aside, fenced off in their own little playpen.

Take Maureen Dowd, who is the excellent White House correspondent for the *New York Times*. She wrote a marvellously funny article about being invited for a social evening at the White House by George Bush, shortly after he had taken office. She described how she'd had to skip a dinner which she'd been greatly looking forward to, how there was no food served, how they were kept waiting by Bush – who had been dining with the British Ambassador – and then taken, for no apparent reason, to a screening room to watch a film about baseball. After that they had been given a tour of the house, including the Lincoln Bedroom where everything, except the phone, is in the correct period style. Bush scratched his head and said: 'It's very austere in here . . . it's a kind of, Victorian kind of thing.'

But this article could not possibly have appeared in the *New York Times*, where it would have been regarded as *lèse majesté* – not at Bush's expense, which wouldn't matter, but at the expense of the news itself, a mystical and almost holy concept to American newspapermen. Instead it appeared in the British paper, the *Independent*, where it told readers far more about the real George Bush than any number of serious and weighty analyses.

Jokes about the news are permitted, but usually on late-night television, where they begin Johnny Carson's *The Tonight Show* and then *Late Night With David Letterman*. These are usually very funny indeed. But even here, the jokes quickly get set in their ways, and become jokes about jokes, like those in England concerning railway sandwiches which went on for years after railway sandwiches had become perfectly edible. Dan Quayle, for example, is universally regarded as stupid. (Marilyn Quayle is in amorous mood, and blows in her husband's ear. 'Thanks for the refill, honey,' he says. On the news of the San Francisco earthquake, Quayle was told to fly to the Epicenter. So he went to Disney World. Quayle thought 'Roe v. Wade', the abortion test case, was the choice Washington faced when he had to cross the Delaware. And so forth, and so on.) In fact, Quayle is a reasonably intelligent fellow, whose greater failing is laziness. But the late-night line is that he is dumb, and nothing will alter that. It would be like declaring Dean Martin to be a teetotaller, or Joan Collins a virgin. Even if these things were true, they couldn't be allowed into the public consciousness; too many jobs depend on them.

FOOD

There are two types of good American food (and America is full of good food): simple, and ethnic. Whatever you do, don't go to those self-consciously American restaurants, or you will wind up eating grilled Mississippi mudfish with Carolina rice and a garnish of fresh Maine scallops and California prunes – a dish like a defence appropriations bill, designed to please as many States as possible and consequently a dog's breakfast, if a dog would eat it, which it might not.

The ethnic food is quite astonishingly varied. Nobody in America simply eats Chinese (well, they might in Muskogee, Oklahoma, but not in a city of any size). You eat Hunan, or Szechuan, or Cantonese. It doesn't even have to be Chinese at all. There's Thai food, and Vietnamese food, and Japanese food, and food from almost every country in the Orient with the possible exception of Australia.

If you want Italian food you might wind up at the kind of place where spaghetti with meatballs marks the limits of the chef's skills, but you can probably find a Tuscan restaurant, or a Sicilian restaurant, or a Roman restaurant or one serving Venetian food, in which everything comes with corn polenta, the Italian-Americans' revenge for grits. Different regions of Mexico have different styles of food, and you can even get Tex-Mex, which, being the Texans' adaptation of Mexican food, is completely phoney and yet has rightly acquired a separate ethnic image of its own.

Eating out in America can be almost unalloyed pleasure. Not everywhere of course. You can be ripped off in New York, and in some of the more obscure States I have had some awful meals involving microwaved hamburgers, a serious abomination. In Idaho, a State which is famous, so far as I can judge, only for the quality of its potatoes (and the virulence of its neo-Nazis, but they are a tiny minority) you are just as likely to get powdered mash extruded from a machine as you are anywhere else.

But the joy of being made welcome! 'Hi, I'm Scott, and I'll be your waiter this evening. If I can tell you about our specials, then I'll be happy to get you folks a cocktail . . .' William Boyd's hero who, on learning the waiter's name, immediately rose to introduce himself, was right. Why not? Other people work for us, whether they are fixing our teeth or our plumbing, and we generally ask their names. Why should waiters and waitresses be regarded as some inferior class of person? A waiter who joined your table, unasked, and began to describe his tangled love-life would be different.

Even the fanciest restaurants in America are generally warm and friendly. In New Orleans one lunchtime we took our two infant children to Commander's Palace, reckoned by some to serve the finest food in North America. The baby had a packet of porridge, and the waiters cheerfully bought hot water to mix with it. Our little girl had a hot dog we had bought in the nearest 7-Eleven. They brought porcelain for her to put it on, silverware for her to eat it with, and jokily asked if the chef had cooked it right. When she asked for vanilla ice-cream they brought a huge silver bowl heaped with the stuff. It never appeared on the bill. Our own delectable four-course meal worked out at less than 10 pounds a head, including drinks. It's time we realized in Britain

that eating out can be good, cheap and most of all delightfully friendly.

Real American food means simple straightforward fare, like hamburgers. This does not mean fast-food burgers, such as those sold in takeaway restaurant chains, which usually have the consistency of industrial cleanser. A real hamburger is made to a simple recipe, for which I am indebted to an article by Alistair Cooke.

You should get the best minced beef you can afford. If all you can see is grey mashed gristle, have the butcher grind up some good stuff. Season with salt and pepper and mould into patties. Add nothing else. You are not making steak tartare. Onion, egg, flour for binding – all are irrelevant. Then grill the burgers. Ideally they should be pink in the middle, but crisp and running with meaty juices on the outside. If in doubt, undercook. You can always sling them back. Only then do you add the garnishes: onion, lettuce, mayonnaise, ketchup, anything you like. (Ketchup plays a central role in American cuisine. Once in Boston, I watched a friend add ketchup to her sliced tomato salad. What startled her most was the fact that I was surprised. But it's quite logical, really. Tomatoes which are grown mainly for colour and texture quite naturally lack tomato flavour, which has to be added.)

There's no law saying that you even need a bun with your burger. Of course, poorer families need to make the meat stretch more, which is why you can still buy a soya product called 'Hamburger Helper' which blends in with the meat. It's said that Nancy Reagan's idea of poverty was finding, in a Bel Air supermarket, a packet marked 'caviar helper'.

Hamburgers are best cooked on an open-air grill, or barbecue. This can be powered by gas, but I prefer regular, old-fashioned charcoal, and use an ancient traditional formula to get it started: pile charcoal in pyramid, soak in charcoal lighter, stand back about a hundred yards and throw a match. When the holocaust dies down (in around half an hour) you should have enough hot charcoal to broil an ox.

Purists will tell you that the odour of the fluid lingers and spoils the taste of the meat. Nonsense. Real men don't eat food so wimpy that it could be tainted by anything short of tear gas. Take spare ribs. These should be back ribs, which have plenty of meat on them. Never buy boneless. A boneless rib is like a leadless pencil. And what would you pick it up with? A fork? What kind of panty-waist are you?

I marinate the ribs overnight in the fridge. The recipe involves two parts of olive oil, one of soy sauce, and a healthy dollop of hoysin, the spicy Chinese sauce. Then grate in plenty of fresh ginger, garlic and spring onions. Or ground cardamom, or cayenne, or 40/20 motor oil, if you so please. Turn the ribs and slather them in the sauce whenever it crosses your mind. In any event, if you feel the need for exact directions, then you shouldn't be cooking ribs.

Give them a half-hour or so in the oven at around 350°F, then crisp them up quickly on the charcoal. Or you can cook them inside a barbecue kettle, very slowly, turning up the heat at the end for the *coup de grace*. Eat with ice-cold, long-neck beers, periodically annoying the neighbours by shouting 'Yee-haw!'

In the South they eat chicken-fried steak, which sounds disgusting, and often is. It's classic poor folks' food, designed to make the cheapest cuts half-edible. You can make it delicious by obtaining first-rate frying steak, such as rib eye. Cut out fat and gristle, then brush with beaten egg. Dredge in well seasoned flour. Repeat. Then fry it in oil which is just short of smoking, until the batter is crisp but the steak inside is still juicy – a few minutes at most.

Chicken-fried steak is served with milk gravy, which is less loathsome than it sounds. Scrape up the fat left from the frying, along with the meat juices and scraps of burnt batter, blend with flour, add plenty of pepper, and let it down with milk. It should not be too stiff. As Tony Hancock said of his mother's gravy, 'At least it used to move around a bit.'

Americans have wonderful desserts. My favourite is brownies: moist, gungy little chocolate cakes. Texture counts for a lot in American food, so the outside should be crisp and crumbly, the inside as soggy as a mud bath, so that the whole thing leaves your mouth caulked with chocolate.

After years of experiment, we have come up with the perfect brownie recipe: (1) buy packet of brownie mix, (2) follow directions. Doing it on your own isn't worth the effort.

Food in America is ritualized far more than in Europe. Of course at Thanksgiving you have to have turkey and squash and other alleged ingredients of the first Thanksgiving dinner. But baseball games and beach barbecues always call for hot dogs. Sitting in a movie theatre, you are almost obliged to eat popcorn. Comfort food is cookies and milk. Breakfast ought to be French toast, which is like a *croque monsieur* without the ham, and, like 'English' muffins, bears no relationship to the cuisine of its alleged country of origin. But French toast is good, and wonderfully simple. Whisk the egg, soak the bread in it, and fry, preferably in butter, unless you are trying to reduce your cholesterol, which you probably are.

The traditional breakfast in America is, sadly, beginning to disappear – or rather, is suffering from the great American skill of preserving the appearance of something valuable without the reality. These days you are likely to be offered the calamitous 'breakfast buffet', which means cold hash browns, soggy bacon and flabby fried eggs gazing up like a mass grave of Cyclops. Watching a true breakfast cook is like watching a conductor pay heed to all parts of his orchestra at once. The potatoes are being flipped. The bacon is scooped up at exactly the peak of crispness and dried in paper towels kept close by for the purpose. His eye is on the sausage and tomato as he turns the egg, over easy perhaps, so that the yolk is still molten, not surrounded by a tough rubbery ring or by slithery uncooked white. Meanwhile, lesser mortals have the task of fixing your toast, butter, juice, jelly and coffee. The cook commands his grill with the casual art of a captain on the bridge.

In Britain we are scared of our food because of the stuff artificially pushed into it. In America people are more frightened of the natural ingredients which lurk there. Saturated fat! Salt! Caffeine! Eating in America resembles how I imagine it was to wait for a poison gas attack during World War Two. You couldn't know what it would be like, only that it would be dreadful. In the old days, foods listed their ingredients on the side of the can. Now they list what they don't contain. 'No Saccharine! Caffeine Free! Lo-Salt! Contains No Nitrates!' a typical can of soda will declare in lettering almost as big as its name. They don't even mention sugar, presumably for the same reason that they don't boast 'Contains No Prussic Acid!' The stuff still tastes like the effluent from Windscale, and is priced at around forty times the cost of its constituent parts, but at least you know that it doesn't contain this month's fashionable poisons.

And there are so many. Look at the lavish produce department at the supermarket. Those burnished red apples are plump and juicy with Daminozide, which may be a carcinogenic. Lethal lettuces are stuffed with Endosulfan, which can cause liver and kidney damage. Tomatoes and cauliflowers may contain Metham-idophos, which can attack the nervous system. The broccoli is sprayed with Parathion, which may be a carcinogenic. So might be Diemthoate, which is sprayed on beans and cabbages – and as for eggs, you might as well swallow hand grenades and wait for the pin to fall out. Beef is full of hormones, so buy too much and the men in your family will grow breasts.

New scares swirl and eddy constantly around the shelves. To eat cheese is to dice daily with death since it contains appallingly high levels of cholesterol. But Cheez Whiz, a yellow substance with a consistency not dissimilar to the scum which forms on washing-up water, contains large quantities of CLA, fatty acids which might actually inhibit cancer.

In the 1980s, cholesterol appeared to replace the Red Menace as the cause of greatest anxiety to most Americans. This was in spite of the fact that there is no proof at all that it is particularly dangerous, and it can be very unhealthy indeed to get your choles-terol level too low. Indeed, it is perhaps the first substance nat-urally produced by the body to be declared a peril to human life. My doctor gave me a long list of what to eat and what to avoid in order to bring my cholesterol level down. On the banned side were hideous, unnatural foods like eggs, cheese, milk and butter. On the allowed side were delicious, natural foods such as margarine, sodas, gelatine desserts and angel food cake.

Someone decided that oat bran helped avoid cancer. So the nation went made for oat bran muffins and oat bran cereals. Then someone else found that some of these contained coconut oil, a lethal producer of cholesterol. Now cereals sometimes proclaim: 'Contains no tropical oils!' Each scare brings solutions which in turn add to the scares.

One of the most puzzling things about America is its beer, specifically why a country which prides itself on the variety and quality of all it produces, should drink a pale fluid which tastes like alcoholic tap water with the flavour removed. Even more baffling is the fact that the two largest ethnic groups in the country, the British and the Germans, came from countries with a long brewing tradition.

In the past there used to be dozens of small, different breweries in every big city, often making beer of innumerable different styles: German, English, Irish, Dutch, Czech and so forth. Over the years, these were all reduced to a single, flabby pilsener beer with too much corn in it. This universal brew is typified by Anheuser-Busch's Budweiser, but it appears as Miller's, Coors', Stroh, and a host of other beers whose sole ambition in life is to resemble Bud.

The imposition of a cheap, nasty, uniform style of beer on an entire nation is one of the greatest triumphs of marketing history. It's as if the French had been persuaded that they only needed to eat pre-sliced processed cheese, or if their vignerons had got together and decided that the only type of wine they would make was a slightly sweet white from an inferior grape, and that the public had better like it because it was all they were going to get.

Ironically, though the French ethnic influence on the United States is only marginal (they tended to emigrate to Quebec), Americans make superlative wines – not only in California, but in New York, Oregon, Washington, and these days even in Texas. Unlike the Medoc, where the better châteaux will not trouble to let you in without advance calls and even letters of introduction, and where the lesser vineyards merely wish to sell you cases of the stuff, in the Napa Valley virtually every grower will welcome you with open arms and open bottles. *Chez* Robert Mondavi, who probably grows a greater range of fine wines than anyone else in America, they will gladly pour the stuff down your throat, with only the merest hint of a sales pitch. A few people are trying to rescue American beer, but the new 'boutique' ales furnish less than 1 per cent of what is sold. Unlike in Britain, where CAMRA arrived in the nick of time, the catastrophe in America has already occurred.

FOUR

A Diffusion of Impotence

During the 1988 presidential election, Michael Dukakis, whom readers may remember as having been the Democratic candidate, was in Iowa campaigning for his party's nomination. He had some advice for farmers there who were suffering difficulties because of government farm support policies. This in itself may seem strange, since the federal government currently pays farmers in Iowa more money to grow unsaleable crops than it spends on its entire foreign aid budget. So instead of producing a surplus of food which people didn't seem to need, Dukakis suggested, why didn't they try something else, such as 'flowers, blueberries and Belgian endive'? 'Belgian endive' is what we call chicory.

It could have been worse. He could have admitted dealing in child pornography. He could have demanded release for the Manson family. On the other hand, it was horrifying enough. His main rival at the time was Richard Gephardt, whose campaign manager immediately realized the enormity of what Dukakis had said. Gephardt quickly ran commercials on TV in South Dakota recalling Dukakis's 'gaffe', ending with the announcer asking, with apparently limitless scorn, 'Belgian *endive*'?

The ad was immediately effective. Straight away, Dukakis staff poured in from Boston to counteract what became known as the 'endive thing'. They produced negative TV ads of their own. It was too late. Dukakis lost South Dakota to Gephardt by an unexpectedly high margin of 44 to 31 per cent. Everyone in both campaigns attributed the result to Belgian endive.

Americans are fond of recalling the war between two Latin American countries which began as the result of a soccer match. Few of them, however, seem especially surprised that their principal election should turn, in part, upon a vegetable. Some naïve folk might even imagine that Dukakis's advice was sound. A check at our local supermarket showed that corn, for example, was fetching around 25 cents a pound while Belgian endive went for 3 dollars, twelve times as much. Dukakis seemed to be offering nothing more than sound capitalist advice along the same lines as 'make fewer quill pens and valve radios!'

This is to misunderstand America and, in particular, the Midwest. Farmers are regarded as a fine and unique breed in the United States. In Europe, we tend to assume that the land has always been there, and farmers are merely the people who happen to have their hands on it at the moment. In the US, it was farmers who did most to create the country out of wilderness. It was their ancestors who piled their belongings into covered wagons, paid what trivial sum they could to buy the virgin territory, and survived the hideous winters to make it fertile. Attack a farmer in England and you can imagine that you're abusing someone who drives a BMW and shoves growth hormones into battery animals. Attack a farmer in the United States and you are assailing the soul of America itself. This is in spite of the fact that the great majority of farm land is now owned by vast agri-business combines whose employees, introduced to a horse, would probably want to know where you put the phone.

Anyhow, the net result is that farmers are regarded as sacrosanct, a little like the apes on Gibraltar. If they go, the implication is, then the country itself crumbles. One of the perks of being a symbol of the nation is that you get to grow whatever you please – if necessary funded by public subsidies. This means planting real, tough, manly crops like corn and soyabeans, not nauseating, wimpy, panty-waisted effeminate vegetation like endives. Short of suggesting that they wear garter belts in the field, or retrain as manicurists, it's hard to think of a notion which would more disgust a red-blooded American farmer.

And it's not just any old endive. It's *Belgian* endive. Many Midwestern farmers are probably unaware of where Belgium is. (There is no Belgian community in the US to speak of, except maybe in Wisconsin: girls with names like Anna-Marie Zwout do not appear as *Playboy* centrefolds and express a wish to go home for some of Mama's delicious Belgian cooking. There are no Belgian bars where glasses of that beer which tastes delicious but looks like sump oil are raised to toast King Baudouin. For this reason, politicians do not have to pay lavish homage to the conception of being Belgian, as they do, say, to the Irish and the Italians.) However, farmers know perfectly well that Belgium is not in America. And if they are asked to grow one foreign vegetable, what fresh humiliations might follow? Italian radicchio? French beans? Chinese gooseberries? Swedes, perhaps? As is well known, Swedes are sex-mad, alcoholic, abortion-loving socialists, who have nothing in common with Midwesterners except a fondness for unpleasant root vegetables.

The endive issue would not go away. It almost became Dukakis's equivalent of Gary Hart's fling with Donna Rice. Dan Quayle, then the Vice-Presidential candidate, went campaigning in Kansas City and thought it would be a neat idea to wave a Belgian endive at the TV cameras so as to illustrate the Democrat's treasonous remarks. He could have shown how the alien plant is even shaped like the heads of those namby-pamby, élitist, Perrier-drinking, foreign salad-munching liberals who were advising Dukakis. Sadly, Belgian endive is nearly as hard to track down in Kansas City as a buffalo might be in Ghent, and no one could find a specimen in time.

But that didn't stop Quayle, who returned to the topic tirelessly. 'The Governor of Massachusetts,' he said in his debate with Lloyd Bentsen, the Democratic candidate for Vice-President, 'he had a farm programme. Grow Belgian endive. That's what he and his Harvard buddies think of the American farmer!'

Endive is a classic example of a political neo-symbol. These days the new, hard school of campaign advisers finds it easy to invent new symbols, often ideas or objects which had no special significance before they were designated as symbols. Massachusetts is a neo-symbol. Quayle never referred to Dukakis by name, but only as 'the Governor of Massachusetts'. This is because the Republicans had decided to decree that Massachusetts was a

symbol of all that is rotten, liberal and unAmerican. (Also because it never votes Republican.)

They started by calling Dukakis a 'Brookline liberal', which didn't really serve, since few people outside the city of Boston have heard of Brookline, though within Boston it has the same ring as 'Hampstead thinker' does in Britain. Then they called him a 'Harvard liberal', which was easier to recognize, but finally they decided to slosh the calumny around the whole State. The Governor of Wisconsin, introducing George Bush at a rally near Milwaukee, referred to Massachusetts as 'that goofy State'. The Boston Tea Party! The Shot Heard Round The World! Paul Revere's Ride! All these events, the mainsprings of the American Revolution, were forgotten. Massachusetts was full of crypto-communist endive eaters, and could be written off entirely. 'The Governor of Massachusetts' was spat out with the venom one might use to accompany a phrase like 'boss of the Albanian Politburo.'

The beauty of symbols is that they simultaneously say less than you want and more than you could. Suppose that Quayle, instead of endlessly repeating the word 'endive', had sneered with curled lip: 'Mr Dukakis says that farmers should stop growing crops for which there is too little demand! He says they should produce crops that command a high price, crops which people want to buy!' This would not have had the intended effect. The symbol avoids the troublesome nuisance of explaining the pros and cons of farm subsidies. It touches the topic without beginning to address it. At the same time it implies that Dukakis is less than fully American, that he is not like the ordinary people he wishes to vote for him.

A symbol will always defeat a statistic. Dukakis had a good record on crime while he was Governor of the hated People's Republic of Massachusetts. Serious crime had fallen by 12 per cent during his spell in office. This was a figure he repeated (though not often, because as an ex-teacher, Dukakis tended to assume that the electorate was taking notes. If he had said it once, there was no reason to say it again. Bush took the view that if you had said it a hundred times, that was a good reason for saying it a hundred times more since it might then get through to any cave-dwelling anchorites who might also have the vote).

Which is why the Bush team needed Willie Horton, the convicted murderer who was released for a weekend furlough in Massachusetts during Dukakis's period as Governor; Horton fled to Maryland where, in a comfortable suburb, he raped a young woman and knifed her fiancé. As a neo-symbol, he was perfect. Best of all, he was black, so awakening hardly dormant fears of Negro rapists appearing in safe white neighbourhoods. The victimized couple campaigned for Bush, though it appeared that what had offended them most was Dukakis's failure to send a letter apologizing for what had happened. This was typical of Dukakis. Since it wasn't his fault, and since an apology wouldn't actually undo the crime, he must have seen little point in sending one.

Again, Horton made it easy for Bush to duck the real issues. Two murderers had murdered again after being released by Ronald Reagan when he was Governor of California. Furloughs actually reduce the crime rate, since convicts who have had a chance to adjust to an unfamiliar world are less likely to return to crime. But the symbol swept away all these arguments. Like a virus injected into the body politic, a symbol destroys any rational argument it meets in its path.

Thanks to the Horton affair, there is scarcely an ambitious Governor left in the United States who will dare to let a convict out before his time is served. The net result may well be that violent men will be released, after twenty-odd years in jail, into a society with which they are entirely unable to cope. Some of them will, no doubt, kill people again. It is highly unlikely that any of these crimes will be blamed upon George Bush and his campaign managers.

It emerged that Bush's choice as Vice-President, Dan Quayle, had avoided service in Vietnam by enlisting in the Indiana National Guard (where his job was to help with public relations, a tougher job than might be thought. All those rubber chicken dinners, all those dreary speeches, all those handouts to the local media. There are few atheists at the Xerox machine). Bush and

96

the Republicans faced a crisis of neo-symbolism. Here was a man who, like the great majority of other middle-class youths in America at the time, had found a way of avoiding combat, but who, unlike the great majority of other middle-class youths at the time, had spoken up noisily in favour of the war. With breathtaking *chutzpah* they decided to make him a neo-symbol of America's military pride. At a National Guard convention he began his speech by barking out his serial number. Bush pointed out that, unlike some, Quayle had never fled to Canada and he 'sure as hell never burned the American flag', which as a qualification for public office is less than impressive, since it would apply to at least 99.999 per cent of all Americans.

The symbol management was, however, perfect. At the end, Quayle was still a national joke. But he was a national joke with guts. By golly, he might not have died for his country, but he would have been prepared to, if ever he had gone to Vietnam, which he didn't, because there was vital photocopying to be done at home. It was a confused message to be sure, but the symbolism was as sharp as ever.

Meanwhile Dukakis stuck with his statistics. Turn on the TV news any night during the election campaign, and there would be Bush with a score of police officers endorsing him. Or else at a flag factory, celebrating increased sales of the American flag thanks to the patriotism inspired by the Reagan years. Dukakis would be on a windswept platform somewhere explaining how the figures proved that his plans for medical care, or college fees, or the defence of the nation, all added up perfectly . . . Sometimes, on a dull day (and there were many), the candidates might be allotted a total of sixty or ninety seconds between them on a national network news. Bush used his fleeting moments to implant yet another symbol in the receptive mind of the electorate, Dukakis to give them just a few of the wide range of exciting statistics bucketing around in his head.

Bush has a tin ear for the English language, but Dukakis couldn't read the American mind. He failed, if you like, to realize that you shouldn't say 'endive' in Iowa. (Oddly enough, George Bush did himself less harm in 1990 when he announced that broccoli would no longer be served on Air Force One, at least less harm with people who happen not to be broccoli farmers. Broccoli is unpopular for quite different reasons than Belgian endive. Refusing to eat broccoli is part of a true American childhood. Belgian endive has no role at all there. But the broccoli incident does illustrate the continuing importance of vegetables in American political life.)

Dukakis's failure to understand symbols ought not to be a disqualification for the presidency, but it is. Many other drawbacks aren't: you can be ugly like Johnson and Nixon, you can be a Roman Catholic like Kennedy, or you can be a chump, like Ronald Reagan. These do not appear to matter. But you have to be able to decipher America's symbols.

You also need to be good on TV. This, like riding a bike, is initially difficult but can be learned. Bruce Babbit, the most engaging of the Democratic candidates, was awful when he started out. Then he took a training course in television speaking, and though he was still awful, he was slightly less awful and no longer looked as if the Pillsbury Doughboy were suffering from Parkinson's Disease. (Babbit also went in for wry, self-deprecating jokes, which amused the press. For example, he asked why people should want to support a 'rag, tag and bobtail army like the Nicaraguan Contras, when they could support my campaign'. Sadly, his jokes didn't amuse the public. The underlying message they seemed to hear was: give him the job, and he'll be wry and deprecating about *us*.) By now everyone believes that in politics, television is all-important. In fact, it is more important even than that. It isn't merely the most important reality; it has replaced reality altogether.

Bishop Berkeley, one of the first Irish-American immigrants, who went to live in Rhode Island in 1728 in an attempt to discover whether culture could be brought to the colonies (perhaps having decided that it couldn't, he returned after three years), once asked, though not in so many words, whether, if a tree fell in the forest and no one was aware of the fact, it could, in any meaningful sense, be said to have fallen. The American politician has a similar fear: if he says or does something, and it fails to appear on the six o'clock news, could it truly be said to have happened at all?

Here's a typical scene in Manchester, the principal city of New Hampshire, where the primary election is critically important for candidates of both parties. Richard Gephardt had won the Iowa Democratic caucuses, not least, as we have seen, by exploiting the matter of the Belgian endive. Two days later he was in the New England snows on his way to an old people's centre. His polls had shown that old people were worried about threats to their social security, or pensions, and that the candidate who convinced them he was on their side would gather a rich harvest of votes.

But at the centre, very few people were even aware of his presence. This is because he had taken up position at one end of the room, chosen because it was flanked by a large gap where the thirty or so representatives of the media could get a clear look. Most of the people at this very table were unable to talk to him or to hear a word of what he said because he wasn't actually talking to them; he was speaking to the boom microphones which just picked up his low relaxed voice. However, the two old people on either side of him were in the shot, and appeared on the six o'clock news that night, when Gephardt was said to have 'visited an old people's center to tell them about his plans for preserving their social security' – or words to that effect. There was the candidate looking friendly and assured with two indubitably old people.

Could he have stayed behind and chatted to the other hundred or so old folk present? Why yes, but what a terrible waste of time that would have been! After all, the sound bite was in the can ready for that night's news. Almost certainly there were urgent fund-raising phone calls to make from his motel room. Why in heaven's name should a candidate spend ten minutes on a solitary voter who might or might not vote for him, when he could be spending the same time on someone who might (or might not) cough up 50,000 dollars – nearly all of which will be spent on TV commercials?

Now that America has reached the era of the permanent campaign, even the winner of an election cannot rest. American foreign policy is as closely geared to the topic of the nightly news as is the discussion on the Belgian endive or the Massachusetts policy on parole. To follow a president abroad is to be part of a massive, four-year-long re-election campaign. At Andrews Air Force Base, south of Washington, you join the press plane, which is generally a 747 of Pan Am. A team of attendants who have served on this flight before, and who are proud of their style – they can be pouring champagne when lesser cabin crew would be urgently strapping themselves in – have been summoned from the airline's whole route network. Wherever you sit on this plane, the service is always first-class, and the White House travel people charge each news organization a hefty, though not unreasonable, price for the considerable privilege of using it.

We flew behind President Bush to attend the funeral of the Japanese emperor, which was due to take place the morning after we arrived. Unfortunately, almost on the other side of the planet, a Senate committee had voted against confirming John Tower, a diminutive lecher from Texas, as Secretary of Defense. For the evening news, this was the only story, and since an American administration is deemed to be wherever the President happens to find himself, Tokyo was where the story was unfolding. No more than a handful of White House correspondents went any-where near the funeral tents on the other side of Tokyo. They may run Japanese royal funerals on average twice a century, but that doesn't cut it on the evening news.

In Poland, the White House had a problem. They had predicted riots in the street when Bush arrived. In their boundless enthusi-asm and love for the President the Polish people might even rise up against their (then) communist masters. The sheer force of Bush's personality could, in itself, create a serious diplomatic embarrassment.

It didn't quite work like that. Bush was politely received in Warsaw, though there was more raw excitement when a consign-ment of sausage appeared at a nearby butcher's shop. This mat-tered because – while Bush's staff could mumble off the record about how the popular enthusiasm for the Pope had reflected support for Solidarity, and now Solidarity was legal – the TV pictures were the wrong sort. The White House wanted joy, dementia, passion. What they got was less excitement than the average High School marching band could engender at home.

(The principal aim of the White House on these occasions is to keep reporters as far away from the President as is possible, given that they are in the same city. This is because reporters merely clutter up the TV picture and sometimes take advantage of their position to ask the President questions for which he has not necessarily been prepared. However, by following the local citizens instead of my fellow journalists, I was able to get within a few feet of him at a memorial for the dead of the Warsaw Ghetto. This meant that I was jammed up against the officer who carries the 'football', the fat black leather briefcase which contains the nuclear launch codes. The 'football', so called because under American football rules the ball must never be dropped, goes with the President everywhere, fixed to the officer's wrist by a leather-covered steel chain. Thus, it could be seen a few feet away from Ronald Reagan when he strolled in Red Square with Mikhail Gorbachev during his visit to the Soviet Union. This produced two splendid absurdities: first, it was highly unlikely that Reagan would decide that *that* was an ideal moment to eradicate Moscow. Secondly, if he had decided to, the codes would have been almost meaningless. The briefcase contains detailed plans for fighting a nuclear war in almost every conceivable situation. If a warning that enemy missiles were on the way had been received, Reagan would have been in the position of someone trying to learn the rules to 'Dungeons and Dragons' in four minutes.)

For Bush, back in Poland, things improved on the second day. The crowd in Gdansk was bigger. It was enthusiastic, at times. People were waving American flags. This was more like it. Never mind that the cheers were louder for Lech Walesa than for Bush. Never mind that Walesa was positively angry about the tiny subvention the Americans proposed to give a reformed Polish government. Back home, the pictures on the news were terrific. The trip had been worth it. Even though no one had the faintest idea of who he would be, the Democratic challenger to Bush in '92 had already been delivered a damaging blow.

All of this leaves us with the question of what a politician does once he has been elected. The answer is that he spends much of his time in office ensuring his re-election. Take the subject of guns.

Hunting is one of the most popular sports in the United States, and consequently millions of Americans possess guns. The US has a *per capita* murder rate which most years is actually worse than Northern Ireland. Around half those murdered, about ten thousand people a year, are killed by handguns, though you are not allowed to suggest that there is any connection between this statistic and the prevalence of gun ownership, or the National Rifle Association will be on to your case in less time than it takes to fire a Saturday Night Special at a liquor store owner. The NRA hunts down any deviation from the true word with the same vigour and determination as Islamic fundamentalists seek blasphemers.

Occasionally I would appear on radio shows and, if the subject came up, took the chance to be offensive about the NRA. It was my own sport of choice. What made it easy was what makes hunting quail so easy; the quarry behaved so predictably. It never failed. The letters would pour in. This did puzzle me a little, since the show I most often appeared on was broadcast by National Public Radio, regarded as an unAmerican service listened to by the kind of people who eat vegetarian quiche. It was hard to know what a red-blooded hunter was doing listening to 'Weekend Edition' on NPR when he could have been behind a tree, waiting for Bambi's mother.

The letters were all much to a pattern, explaining how the Constitution bestowed on all Americans the right to bear arms (sometimes this was linked in a faintly alarming way to the fact that it was the British they were originally supposed to bear arms against) and how it was a jungle out there, would I like it if drug-crazed muggers came into my house to rape my wife and kidnap my children? Then, inevitably, there would be a lyrical section in which the writer listed all the weaponry he himself possessed. (This was inevitable for 'sporting' purposes or else as part of a prized collection. Gun-collectors always talk about their 'hobby' as if, in some mysterious way, amateur pursuits should be exempt from any social obligations. I can't imagine philatelists getting such privileged treatment if their chosen pastime indirectly led to the deaths of thousands of people a year.) At some point in the letter, every detail of each firearm the writer possessed would be lovingly described, at such length that it assumed an almost pornographic quality. He would wind up with a coda on the nature of freedom, with the implication that if the police were allowed seven days to check on the identity of someone who wanted to buy a field piece, maybe a Bofors gun or a heat-seeking missile, then the Kremlin might as well take over now without wasting any time.

This means that it is incredibly easy to buy guns – at least in some States. Go into a store in say, Texas, and you might hear a conversation roughly along these lines:

Customer: I'd like to buy an Uzi sub-machine-gun, please.

Gun-shop owner: Sure thing. Here it is. And we have a special on ammunition this week!

Customer: Will you take an out-of-State cheque?

Gun-shop owner: No problem, provided you got three separate pieces of picture ID, plus two major credit cards, your birth certificate, social security card, a Freedom of Information act print-out of your FBI file and if you'll leave your first-born with us until the cheque clears.

Some Americans (though by no means all; every opinion poll shows that most support more curbs on gun ownership) are puzzled why we foreigners are puzzled by their fascination with firearms. I used to ask how they would feel about a country where people were equally obsessed with, say, nitric acid. You'd have spokesmen for the National Acid Association warning that there are thousands of acid-throwing criminals out there, and that law-abiding citizens need plenty of acid to stop their own faces from being flayed.

There'd be full-page ads in popular magazines, showing decent folk holding up little brown bottles of acid. 'It's every American's right to a hobby,' the caption would read. 'Mine is making copper etchings of the Grand Canal and other picturesque scenes to give as welcome Christmas and birthday presents. That's why I keep a vat of nitric acid at home. Y'know, there's a bunch of fancy-pants liberals up in Congress who want you to believe that's dangerous. Well, I'm here to tell you that only one of our neighbors' children has ever fallen in . . .'

The National Acid Association would denounce regulatory laws as 'A Charter For Criminals', declaring that no American could feel truly free unless he could buy a bottle of the stuff, off the shelf, at any all-night 7-Eleven store whenever he or she pleased. A snappy new slogan would be coined: 'Acid doesn't rip away skin, exposing the raw flesh beneath; people do.' Finally, a bill which would have slowed down the sale of acid to convicted acid-throwers would be tossed out of the Congress, a decision hailed as a victory for truth, freedom and the American way.

Of course that's utterly absurd, but it is precisely the basis on which gun laws are fashioned in the US. The National Rifle Association has become a bureaucracy on its own, with an annual budget bigger than some medium-sized cities. Like all bureaucracies, its principal task is its own preservation. Every year it disburses some 70 million dollars, much of which goes into the pockets (or 'election funds' as we are supposed to call them) of legislators who might be disposed to vote the right way.

In order to keep this money flowing in, it has to create continuous scares among its supporters, arguing, for example, that if there were to be restrictions on hand-held bazookas, the limp-wristed liberal élite would next want to ban all guns, with the result that American men would have to sit at home doing needlework while psychopathic Mexicans were piling in through the back door.

The arguments they marshal against almost any restrictions have a fascinating, rococo quality. Assault rifles, for example, which have marginal sporting use but have been employed to mow down schoolchildren in playgrounds, are necessary for the humane killing of deer, which might otherwise die a slow and agonizing death from a puny rifle bullet. The problem here is that a direct hit with an AK-47 would be likely to scatter the deer over a large part of the county, thus making it of little use either for its skin or its meat, or even as a trophy, unless you want to hang an inch of antler on your wall next to half a tail.

The NRA's skill has been to realize that most legislators don't care very much about anything, except for their own re-election. Every lawmaker, in the House or Senate, will have his pet topics, and tightening gun restrictions is a favourite for quite a few. But they're still a small minority and they only have one vote each. The trick is to bring up a dumpster full of money to every member who has no strong opinions either way. Most of them are so desperate to get hold of cash to ensure re-election that they will take it from almost anyone – and willingly vote the right way as a consequence.

The system is brilliantly effective. In 1988, the House had to consider a modest enough amendment – the one which would have obliged gun buyers to wait seven days before collecting their purchases while the police checked them out. The amendment was tossed aside. Of the 228 members who voted against it, no fewer than 193 had received money from the NRA.

Which leaves us with the question of why so many members require so much money. You don't have to spend very long out in the sticks to find the answer.

Take a Senate race in a small State. The place may have a population of less than a million, but it has as many senators as California, which is to say two, and they carry just as much clout in Washington. Happily for them, it doesn't cost a great deal to get ads on TV, since the spending power of, say, Bismarck, North Dakota, is a great deal less than that of Chicago or San Francisco, so a minute in prime time costs roughly what would buy you a few seconds in Los Angeles. The candidates take this as an invitation to buy even more advertising time. The net effect, if you have to live there, is ghastly. Watching TV is like attending some terrible dinner party at which the hostess has foolishly invited two people who are involved in a feud with each other, a feud which they pursue in spite of every attempt to change the subject.

There you are, innocently watching *The Cosby Show*, and during the break an old lady appears. 'Did you know that Chuck Tweedledee voted against bills which would have improved social security payments for us old folk, five times? I don't think us retired people can afford Mr Tweedledee, do you?' A message appears at the bottom of the screen: 'Paid for by the Friends of Mel Tweedledum.'

Ten minutes later there's another break. This time we get to hear from Chuck himself. 'You know, friends, my opponent has been telling lies about my record on social security. I know the people of this State are too smart to believe these lies. But for the record I have voted 8,276 times for bills which would increase social security payments for the old folk who have worked all of their lives to make our country great.

'And you should know that my opponent voted for a bill which would have made child pornography legal. As the father of three wonderful children, I don't think we can afford to have a man like that represent us in Washington.' The message: 'Paid for by the Friends of Chuck Tweedledee' scrolls along the bottom of the screen.

Of course it's all nonsense. The votes 'against' pensions were minor amendments to vast portmanteau bills; perhaps each one made a few dollars' difference a year to a handful of people. Or perhaps not. Nobody cares about the details. The picture of a man who delights in the thought of old ladies dying because they can't afford heat, while he flies to the Caribbean for a golf vacation, is a vivid and commanding one. No wonder that the victim has to produce an equally distorted reply. The alleged support for child pornography may mean that he once voted against some nutty bill, introduced purely for publicity purposes, which would have imposed mandatory life imprisonment on the owners of news stands who displayed a tit and bum magazine in which one of the young women pictured was aged seventeen and not eighteen.

The struggle goes on until the last minute. Tweedledee produces his mother to swear that her son, whom she has known for forty-seven years, would never do anything to harm old people. Tweedledum declares that his opponent is a 'drug abuser'; it turns out that he once admitted smoking a joint in college, like every other student in the 1960s, except those at the fundamentalist

Oral Roberts University in Tulsa, and no doubt some of them as well.

All this requires money. Huge sums of money. A full-scale Senate election can now cost 20 million dollars. The effect is that legislators no longer campaign in order to have the privilege of serving in public office. They serve in public office in order to be able to continue campaigning. It is a precise inversion of democracy.

Senator Jesse Helms is a classic instance. The hard-line fruit-cake right-winger from North Carolina continually espouses hard-line fruitcake causes – such as preventing the creation of Martin Luther King Day – not because they have any hope of success, but because they bring enough publicity to ensure the flow of money from wealthy, hard-line fruitcakes. This money is sufficient to secure his re-election, often by narrow margins, so that he can continue to pursue hard-line, fruitcake causes.

One effect is that government is increasingly being supplanted by public relations. This is not exactly an original observation, and much has been written about it. What is not perhaps realized is the way that PR has entered every realm of government. Doing wonderful things is now far less important than persuading the public that you are doing wonderful things.

Take the Pentagon, or Department of Defense. It shares much in common with the NRA, being an unwieldy bureaucracy with too much money to spend, largely devoted to its own survival. In the recent absence of a truly threatening enemy, the Soviet Union having apparently decided to vacate the role for the time being, this depends largely on a blend of blackmail and public relations.

The blackmail is easy. While the Cold War was still in effect, the annual sum spent on defence in the United States was around 300 billion dollars, which is nearly 3,000 dollars per household, and which means that, put another way, the average American worker hasn't finished paying for his share of missiles, aircraft carriers and tanks until early March each year. This money is spent all over the country. The Pentagon is now the opposite of the Amway corporation. It has set itself up as the world's first pyramid *buying* scheme.

It is almost impossible to close any military base in any place at any time, even if it was originally established to guard against the British threat in the War of 1812, since this would lead to a loss of jobs in the relevant State and hence to the nightmare of a congressman's opponent declaring in his TV ads that he 'did nothing to save the Benedict Arnold Army Base for our State'. Almost everyone is firmly in favour of reduced expenditure on defence. Almost nobody is in favour of reduced expenditure on defence in their home State or district.

Similarly with procurement. Any big system, like the Strategic Defense Initiative, will be spread over as many States and through as many congressional districts as is possible. A congressman can know rationally that, for example, the first fully computerized horse-shaped armoured personnel carrier designed for infiltration behind enemy defences is a nonsense, which would involve spending the equivalent of the Gross National Product of some medium-sized countries in pursuit of an uncertain and possibly non-existent gain. But the fact that a crucial plastic grommet for EPIC (the Equine Personnel Infiltration Carrier; the Pentagon loves acronyms) is manufactured in his State transforms him into an attack dog, patrolling the project's perimeter fence, determined that not a penny of federal money shall be filched from his electorate.

At some point, however, the public has to be brought into the loop, and this is where the press plays its part. Can you conceive of phoning up, say, Aldermaston nuclear weapons research laboratory in England, announcing yourself as a foreign reporter, and asking if you can come round to take a look? The chances are that the only reason the person you spoke to didn't hang up immediately was that he wanted to give the Special Branch time to trace the call and have you arrested.

Yet when I phoned the Lawrence Livermore Laboratory near San Francisco and made much the same request, the reply was roughly along these lines: 'When can you get here?'

Of course, there is a price. Like those time-share salesmen who offer you a toaster or a cheap holiday if you'll come and listen to their spiel, you do have to endure a lengthy sales pitch, chiefly

about the miracle of SDI and how, while it wouldn't actually
protect any big cities from being struck by nuclear weapons (a
warhead is a conical shape, so that if you looked up at the right
moment, just before the airburst, you would imagine that life on
earth was about to be ended by a falling ice-cream) it would at
least discourage the Russians or whoever from trying. The popular
notion of SDI was as a sort of umbrella over the populace. The
Pentagon's idea was an umbrella over their missiles.

On another occasion I asked to visit Strategic Air Command,
the base in Nebraska from which a nuclear war would actually be
fought, though not for long, since SAC itself would be wiped out
in the first wave of missiles. It is thus one of the few establishments in the history of warfare whose principal role is to retaliate
for its own destruction.

The staff there could not have been more welcoming if they
had been a car dealership and I had expressed an interest in a new
Cadillac. Indeed, the tone was almost identical. There's a big sign
over the gate at SAC labelled 'Peace is our Profession', a form of
words faintly reminiscent of the Kray Twins' description of their
business as 'protection'.

In the briefing rooms they have pictures of missiles. American
missiles and planes are set against beautiful mountain scenery or
golden sunsets, whereas Soviet missiles sit under lowering clouds,
as if they had just been wheeled out from hangars in Hell. An
army captain spent an hour explaining to me, with the help of
impressive visual aids (any graph marked 'Secret' would usually
consist of four inexplicable red lines) how it was essential that
America's rockets should be mounted on special trains which, in
the event of a war being threatened, would move at random around
the rail system making it impossible for the other side's missiles
to find them and so preventing a Soviet first strike.

I wondered aloud whether this might not actually turn a
run-of-the-mill crisis into a nuclear war, since the enemy, knowing that the US missiles were about to reach safety, might be
inclined to let their own rip before they were made useless. The
captain gave me a strange yet somehow patient look, rather like
a car dealer who thinks he is about to make a sale, but has just

been asked what those four round things are at the corners. I realized that this essentially metaphysical argument about the course of a nuclear crisis was irrelevant. The entire point about the rail-based missile system is that it costs a stupendous amount of money. It needs no other justification.

In the end, I got my reward, the equivalent of the toaster, and was taken into the Command Center, an enormous room which you have probably seen several times in the movies. It's where the hot line to the President is waiting, and where the general in charge would arrange for the nuclear launch codes to be sent to silos round the Midwest. (Periodically, the war heads are returned to California to be checked out. Meanwhile, the actual bombs are stored in bunkers near their silos. In Rapid City, South Dakota, I met a retired plumber called Harold, one of whose jobs had been repairing the sprinkler system in these bunkers which, he said, was always going wrong. This was not encouraging.)

I had half-expected a red button somewhere labelled 'The Big One', but of course there wasn't. However, you could see the immense 15 foot screens at the front of the room which would chart the progress of a war second by second. When I arrived, one of them carried this message: 'Welcome, Simon Haggart, London Observer.'

I turned to the colonel who was showing me around and mumbled, in my British way, that it as all very flattering, but what would the screens normally have shown?

'Normally,' he said, 'we'd try to spell your name right.'

It is all a matter of public relations. Members of Congress increasingly vote in such a way as to obtain money from wealthy companies in order that they can run TV ads saying how wisely they have voted. The Pentagon raises money not so much to defend America – that job could be performed for a fraction of the cost – but to preserve its own existence, in which respect it closely resembles the NRA.

These days congressmen (some of whom spend up to four hours a day in fund-raising) do not generally vote as their constituents would wish; they vote in such a way as to raise money in order to be able to claim that they have voted as their constituents

110

would wish. Like Bishop Berkeley's falling tree, a record of honourable public service might as well not exist if you have no means of boasting about it. In these days when a political rally means millions of people sitting at home watching the same TV commercials, that costs an enormous sum of money. The congressman is trapped in an endless cycle. Fund-raising has become a form of chain letter, making a few people immensely rich at the expense of the suckers – in this case the rest of the population.

So is the President caught in a similar net. With breathtaking cheek, George Bush fought in 1988 partly against his opponent's record on the environment. However, when he won office, Bush became strangely lukewarm on such topics as acid rain and global warming. The reason was that the big corporations whose money he would need for re-election did not wish to spend the massive sums required to reduce pollutants. Bush had a choice: either to safeguard the environment, or instead to let it go hang and use the funds thus raised to persuade people that he had safeguarded the environment. The choice was easy; perhaps inevitable.

For two hundred years, the US has been rightly proud of the 'separation of powers', the system which keeps the administration, the legislature and the judiciary rigidly apart. The modern demands of the permanent campaign have, however, replaced this with something more damaging: the diffusion of impotence.

FIVE

Frightening the Horses

The United States is simultaneously the most prudish and the most sexually liberated nation on earth. How is it that in some States you can buy – off the shelf – a magazine which describes or even depicts in as much detail as a medical textbook practices which, followed in the privacy of your own marriage, are actually illegal? In Georgia, for example, you can go to jail for having oral sex with your spouse. Indeed one man, tricked by a wife who wanted both a divorce and her revenge, found himself in prison recently for exactly that.

Yet Georgia's principal city, Atlanta, is proud of its seventeen strip clubs, which it believes are the finest in the land. It may be right.

Purely in the interests of journalistic inquiry, I went with a small party to the Cheetah III, which isn't really a club but an upmarket bar. The place was decorated in shiny marble and mirrored glass, as if Nebuchadnezzar had got the Hyatt Regency contract. You pay 5 dollars to get in, and an enormous man, built to the same plans at Mount McKinley, shows you to a table. The waitresses are all fully dressed, and charge normal bar prices.

There is a dress code – long trousers, shirts with collar – but naturally that applies only to the customers. Most of these are in suits and 'power' ties (in those days that meant yellow silk), and have clearly called in on their way home from the office. Most have that confident, macho style favoured by American businessmen. There are even one or two women.

And all around are girls, eight or ten at a time, dancing to the rock music, on the bars, the tables and the cat-walks, each and every one, as they say here, 'nekkid as a jaybird'. (Or almost so.

One oddity is that many of the girls realize that they look more beguiling in something, even in one case a kind of woolly leotard. Three who *were* naked nevertheless kept their glasses on. It seems to be a new fetish; how sad that Dorothy Parker did not live to see it.)

The girls ranged from very good-looking indeed to astoundingly beautiful. The reason why they work here is that they can earn a great deal, and it would be hard to make the connection between sex and money more explicit. Each girl has a garter around the top of her right thigh, and if she's been dancing on a table, the customer who invited her over is expected to tuck in a tip. The consequence is that by the end of their shift, they appear to have cabbages of cash strapped to the top of their legs. Freud would have had little problem analysing this.

The customers were young – very few were over forty – and while there were no shouts or lewd wolf-whistles, there were no furtive silences either. They looked chatty, at ease, no more guilty than they would in any other kind of bar.

A businessman who was sharing our table asked one girl over to dance. She climbed up on to the table, then handed him her underthings, in a matter-of-fact fashion, as if he were her husband helping her change for a swim. Then she danced in her high heels and smiled engagingly at us. I thought it courteous to leave a gratuity, and while she had her back to me, fumblingly tried to push the money into her garter.

'Oh, sir,' she said, 'yew cain't do it from behind.' This, she explained, was not because patrons might steal the cash, but because they might try to dig their hands in for quite different reasons. The three gigantic bouncers, or 'floor managers', would be straight over for a little chat, on a man-to-mouse basis.

The shame! The mortification! Why is it horribly more embarrassing to break a code of which you are completely unaware than to do wrong knowingly? Suddenly I was back at some child's birthday party, red-eyed after being reproached for transgressing another family's house rule. Why could they not put large placards at the entrance: 'Patrons are requested not to do it from behind'?

At eight o'clock the night shift takes over, and for a spell all

the girls dance together. So for fifteen minutes we were surrounded by sixty gorgeous naked women jiggling up and down. This is something which very few people experience in a lifetime, and certainly not for a mere 5 dollars. On the cat-walk was one of the most beautiful women I have ever seen, before or since. The disc jockey said: 'Now, remember, fellas, the girls cannot ask themselves to your table. You gotta *ask* them. A two-dollar tip is more than enough!' I invited her over, though my attempts to wink in a casual, old hand kind of way probably made her suspect that I suffered from the kind of nervous tic one would expect in a pervert. She came anyway, and demurely put out a hand to be helped up on to the table. She passed me her slip and began to dance.

All four of us round the table smiled politely. It seemed the only response. In between steps she would chat, like a dentist's receptionist slotting things into your mouth: 'So you guys are all reporters, huh?' and 'How d'you like Atlanta?' I wondered why I wasn't aroused. Captivated, for sure; who wouldn't be by such extraordinary beauty? I suppose the answer is that the most erotic moments are those which bring the promise of things to come. 'Your place or mine?' uttered by a woman in an anorak and snow boots is more exciting than nakedness in the most beautiful girl who, if you were to lay the lightest finger upon her person, would have three human grizzlies pull you to pieces like an overcooked chicken.

I didn't tour all American cities looking for strip clubs, but civic pride counts for a lot in the US, so when I mentioned Cheetah III to a friend in Houston, she bridled. In Houston, she said, they had a *much* better strip joint. Indeed it was the place which had given Atlanta the idea. It was called Rick's, and she would arrange for me to visit.

The principal difference is that in Rick's, the girls are expected to perform a 'lap dance', which is, I surmise, an American invention designed to give the customer the maximum erotic charge without actually breaking the law. It is, you might say, sexual intercourse without the intercourse bit. The girl sits on your lap, naked except for a G-string, and for the period of one record on the sound system, wriggles and jiggles like the spider swallowed by Burl Ives's old lady, gazing at you the while with the adoration one might lavish upon one's father who had been thought long lost at sea. At least that's what Jodi did to me. All this is for a tip ranging from 10 dollars in the daytime to 25 dollars at night (up to around 8 p.m. is the 'happy hour', though not so-called).

The law is specific. Reproductive organs must remain twelve inches apart at all times. If patrons let their hands stray near the moving parts, then the girls are instructed to take the hands in their own while fondling them, thus giving the impression that they are overcome with yearning in order to cover up for the fact that they're not. Occasionally members of the Houston Police Department vice squad visit Rick's and monitor the activities there. I gather it is a popular assignment. One Japanese visitor, unaware of what the owners call the 'Rick's Concept', reached out and touched. His feet barely touched the ground as he left. After all, what kind of filthy foreign maniac imagines that he can be within twelve inches of unclothed pulchritude and actually want to get closer? She may be sitting on your lap, her pillowy bosom inches from your popping eyes, but she is in really further from you than any *Playboy* centrefold.

The co-owner of Rick's is a Canadian called Robert Watters, who was educated at the London School of Economics. He explained that the girls actually pay 25 dollars a night to work there, since the more hard-working could easily take home 700 dollars a night in tips. It's possible to be a member of Rick's, or at least have a season ticket, on a sliding scale which indicates status in the burlesque world, rather like American Express green, gold and platinum cards. Indeed, the impression you're given is that it's just another business expense. You owe yourself membership of Rick's, you've worked hard to have those girls half your age squirming around and gazing at you with near incestuous lust, as if, were there no bouncers around, they would have your pants round your ankles before you could stop them.

I asked Robert Watters if there was anything he had learned at the LSE which had helped him to learn how to run an upmarket strip club. 'Everything I learned at the LSE,' he replied. Later he took me on a tour of the dressing-rooms. I reflected that when I was a schoolboy, it would have been impossible to think of any more thrilling fantasy than this. So why was it a disappointment? Perhaps for the obvious reason: in a strip club, or 'burlesque restaurant', the dressing-room is the only place where the girls have their clothes *on*.

It's customary, in articles about strip clubs, to say that they are sad places. I didn't think so. The atmosphere struck me as jolly and upbeat. The lush décor implied to the clients, I suspect, money and hence respectability. The beauty of the girls, the lavishness of the surroundings, had the same function as their expensive suits and ties: 'You've worked for this,' they murmured, 'you fully deserve to enjoy it. Guilt? Guilt is for losers.' Both Houston and Atlanta are set inside rural States with a strong Protestant and puritan ethic. So the whiff of immorality was important. Such a club would be pointless in New York, where sin is not a topic people spend much time troubling themselves with, and where there's little repression for people to react against. Yet this has to be denatured sin, sin made decent, sin with a tear-off tab to be kept for inspection at an Internal Revenue audit. At both places I was reminded of – and this will sound peculiar – Penguin Encounter, the exhibit at Sea World in San Diego, where dozens of real penguins live enclosed in a giant glass case along with rocks, ice, dead fish and guano. It's kept at a constant 20°F. You can gaze at the penguins all you want. You can even imagine you're in the Antarctic. But you're not, nowhere near, and in the same way you are 12,000 miles away from having real sex at Rick's.

Here's another scene. It's Friday night at Dupont Circle, Washington, a neighbourhood half a mile north of Downtown. It's a pleasantly raffish area. A few blocks to the east, the city's celebrated drug markets begin. To the west is Kalorama, one of the most expensive areas for real estate on the entire North American continent. We're in the local video rental store, and the man in front of us is clearly in some professional trade: a lawyer, I would guess, since so many people in Washington are. He has a shopping bag from Larimer's, an expensive and well-stocked grocery store which has one of the few butcher's counters where you can see the meat before it's wrapped in cling film. In America, that means upmarket. Our man is taking out a selection of videos. He's got Danny DeVito's *War of the Roses*, a black comedy. He's got *Cinderella*, no doubt for his daughter. But if we crane our head (while trying to make it look as if we've just got a crick) we can see his third selection, which is titled *Lust in the Fast Lane*. This is not the kind of film which gets reviewed by *Les Cahiers du Cinema*, or even *People* magazine. Heavens, what kind of weekend is he planning? The answer is, in his view, a perfectly respectable one. The little girl watches her Disney; in the evening, after dinner, he and his wife enjoy the DeVito, then later they watch the lovely Traci Lords in one of her starring roles as the kind of girl who not only can't say no, but wouldn't want to even if she could. And if that inspires them to try out some of Traci's more gymnastic positions, so be it. Nobody in Britain (at least nobody over the age of about nineteen) thinks anything of going into Boots the Chemist and asking for a packet of condoms, and nobody thinks that Boots shouldn't have them on display. Our American feels much the same about his dirty movie.

When she was a porn star, Traci Lords was at the top of her profession. Most actresses use their faces to express themselves to the audience. Traci was unfettered by these restrictions, and could employ to most eloquent effect every aspect of her body, especially the pink parts. For long stretches her face did not appear at all; rather the camera would concentrate on a few square inches of her, juxtaposing it with a similar acreage of the leading man, allowing the *auteur* to focus his whole attention on the ins and outs of their relationship. Traci's achievement was all the more remarkable since she had little verbal material to work with. Some of her scripts must have been a page long, at most, though why should she need mere language when a final 'Uh uh uh, aiee!' could convey as much emotion to the audience as a whole soliloquy from *Hamlet*?

The problem was that fifteen is a trifle young to be a porn star. When it turned out that dozens of Traci's films were made before her eighteenth birthday, the porn industry went berserk and pulled all her videos – hundreds of thousands of copies of them – off the shelves. (There are no firm figures about who watches porn, but one poll had 40 per cent of VCR owners admitting that they had rented at least one hard-core cassette, and around a hundred new films are churned out every year.) Back in 1989, a Los Angeles dealer was convicted of trafficking in child porn, that is, Traci videos. The gist of his defence was that she had been at it for years, so how was he to know that she was under eighteen? The judge didn't agree. Traci, as the victimized party, went off to Paris to resume her career there, making similar films in which the dangly bits belonged to Frenchmen, and giving new meaning to the phrase 'a frog in the throat'. At the age of twenty-one she was back in the US, making straight films such as *Cry Baby*, in which she appeared as a virgin, unploughed territory indeed.

Every country's obscenity laws seem baffling to those abroad. Up to the age of seventeen years and 364 days, Traci was an innocent child, dragged into a vile criminal trade. Twenty-four hours later she was a mature woman, protected by the steel armour of the First Amendment, which guarantees the right of free speech, even when that speech consists of little more than lavishly illustrated grunts.

The cliché about porn is that it's boring, which is nonsense. It's meant to be stimulating, and it is. That's why people get X-rated movies out of video shops. The girls are all beautiful with fabulous boil-free figures (unlike the blotchy stars of erotic schoolboy favourites from the Jacey, Piccadilly Circus, such as *Some Like It Nude* and *Danish Dentist on the Job*). The men are seedier, indeed are sometimes distinctly plump, or possessed of the kind of moustache which, on a salesman, would make you decide to try another used car lot. But they are paid much less than the women, and in any event, there must be something which allows us to look down on them. After all, they are much better equipped in one department than the majority of us, and have enough stamina to make a Brahmin bull raise a quizzical eyebrow.

The plots and conventions are as fixed as a Noh play and, so to speak, as rigid. Boy meets girl leads to only one thing, rarely preceded by a cup of coffee, never mind a trip to the movies and a decent meal out. Every bout ends improbably in coitus interruptus, since the 'cum-shot' is thought essential and is highly prized.

Plots tend to be somewhat samey. Here's a selection:

Woman orders a pizza. Pizza boy comes round. They copulate.

Woman finds that her Jacuzzi is out of order. Jacuzzi repairman comes round. They copulate.

Woman wants to find out where her errant husband goes in the afternoons. Private detective comes round. They copulate.

There is some variety. Sometimes she copulates with two men. Sometimes she and a friend copulate with one man. Sometimes a lot of people copulate together. Once or twice a woman will copulate with a man who is playing her son, even though he is clearly five years younger than her at most. Usually there will be a lesbian scene, though never one involving male homosexuals, except in speciality videos know in the trade as 'bi'. Now and again, there's a weird and faintly disturbing scene in which the two people who copulate are meant to be married. Of course, that's thought highly exotic and you don't see a lot of it. I don't know but there may well be a special counter in some stores: 'Married'. Men could shuffle up and say: 'Well, I've seen all your stuff. Are you sure you don't have something, er, a little more, er, "matrimonial"?'

Many anti-porn campaigners were hoping that the Traci Lords case would enable them to get laws which banned the distribution of pornographic videos, even those featuring performers over the age of eighteen. However, the law in Los Angeles says that for something to be banned, it must 'violate community standards' and, as the judge in the Traci case argued, you have to be up pretty early in the morning to violate any standards at all in LA.

I find it hard to be terribly exercised about all this. In many ways it seems to me that in public displays of sexuality, the United States has got it about right – or at least not all that dreadfully wrong. Quite simply, sex is not allowed where it might be seen by people who don't want to see it, and given the puritan tradition in the United States, there are plenty of those. Thus there are few nude beaches – so far as I know – unlike southern Europe, in which there are very few stretches of sand where a woman would feel able to wear both pieces of her bikini, on the grounds that it would be more shameful to imply you had something to hide by covering it up. There are certainly no 'Page 3' girls in the newspapers, where the nearest approach to nudity is the matronly women wearing practical underwear in the department store ads. Sex hardly appears on TV, except as the sniggering 'when did you last make whoopee outdoors?' of *The All New Newly-Wed Game* or the nasty obligatory rape scene in many thrillers. There was a great kerfuffle when a character in *thirty-something* (don't those lower case letters set your teeth on edge?) said something to the effect that he was fetching a contraceptive; the fuss implied that normal sex between married couples was a furtive thing which should not even be mentioned on screen.

On the other hand, anyone who wants to see beautiful naked women dancing or wants to watch the sexual act in greater detail than even the participants can see, knows precisely what to do. It'll be offered like any other business transaction. It will not be particularly subtle. On the other hand it will be, by its own lights, straightforward – which is more than your London club with its 25-pound gooseberryade would know how to be.

It would be absurd to suggest that the American attitude to sex – or, at least, to public displays of sex – was universally sensible. No country, especially so huge a country, could possibly have a uniform, enlightened attitude to something so mysterious, so guilt-laden and so capable of creating misery as well as joy. It's shameful, I think, that the subject can hardly be discussed in an open manner on TV (and it took years for individual TV stations to agree to take condom ads, as a means of reducing the transmission of AIDS. Many still won't).

It's also horrifying that in some States private behaviour between consenting adults can also be the subject of criminal prosecution (though of course these 'offences' rarely come to light, except as part of matrimonial disputes, such as that one in Georgia). On the whole, though, the United States seems to get by rather well on the Mrs Patrick Campbell principle: 'Does it *really* matter what these affectionate people do – so long as they don't do it in the street and *frighten the horses*!'

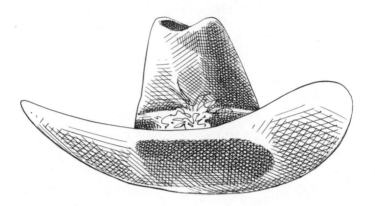

SIX

When the Going Gets Tough

Americans are fascinated by their own love of shopping. This does not make them unique. It's just that they have more to buy than most other people on the planet. And it's also an affirmation of faith in their country, its prosperity and limitless bounty. They have shops the way that lesser countries have statues. When the superlative Union Station was rebuilt in Washington, what did they choose to stuff it with? Dozens of shops, of course. They're the first thing many visitors see when they arrive in the nation's capital, proud symbols of America's majesty. The Capitol is what you see next.

They must be the world's most self-conscious shoppers. You can buy jokey keyrings saying 'Shop Till You Drop', or T-shirts printed with 'When the Going Gets Tough, the Tough Go Shopping'. The term 'bag ladies', meaning homeless women, derives from the shopping bags they carry all their possessions in. By contrast, for an unhomeless (or 'homed') woman, the correct label on the bag can greatly enhance her social status. Some of the fancier shops will sell you a paper carrier bag with their own name on it for as little as one dollar, so you can have the privilege of paying to be their walking advertisement. Bags from Korvette and Wal-Mart are free, but some people prefer to take their Neiman-Marcus bag along and put the goods in that, so that acquaintances at the bus stop can say, 'My sakes, I had no idea than Neiman-Marcus carried pink polyester housecoats!'

Shopping is done at the mall. A typical mall covers an area roughly the size of Liechtenstein, and has nearly as many stores. Some of the shops are huge, sprawling round the mall and taking over other, lesser, shops, like the Third Reich. Others are tiny little shops within shops where you can obtain necessities such as mango-juice shakes, or fake sepia photographs of yourself dressed in nineteenth-century costume. These can be identified by window displays showing people wearing bustles together with those modern spectacles which look as if the earpieces have been fitted on upside down.

On arrival at the mall, your first job is to find somewhere to park. On a weekday this will be easy. At the weekend, it won't. Naturally you don't want to join the line of cars circling the mall in the pathetic hope of finding a space just at the moment someone is leaving it. Instead you spot a couple carrying a clutch of shopping bags towards their car and follow them, like a kerb-crawler. It's a good tip to use your 5 m.p.h. collision bumpers to nudge them gently on the back of the calf, as a friendly hint that you haven't got all day. Then, on arriving at their car, they will stuff the parcels into the trunk and return to the shops for more, pausing only to wave a middle finger cheerily in your direction, the traditional sign that they'll be back in just one minute.

Once inside, you see long queues everywhere. 'Wait a minute,' you think, 'this isn't GUM, the notorious Moscow department store in which people join five-hour lines when word gets out that a consignment of plastic shoes has just arrived from Tbilisi.' And you're right. There is plenty of merchandise. It's all around you. If you were that kind of person it would be quite easy to hoist a microwave oven on to your shoulder and make for the exit, or rather it would be if the goods weren't tagged with electronic security devices which, if not removed by the sales assistants, would render you sterile within two days. The catch is that the queues are for the assistants. In Russia they have a surplus of people to sell goods which don't exist. In America they have a surfeit of goods but no one to sell them.

Even when you do find an assistant it takes another fifteen minutes to buy the stuff. This is because nowadays the store does its stocktaking in your time instead of its own. The assistant has to key in the stock number and innumerable other digits relating to you and your personal life. The codes are quite literally longer than those required to launch a nuclear missile. After that, your credit card may be flourished. (This is not always an easy process, either. Once, at Neiman-Marcus in Houston, I tried to buy a sweater with an American Express card. Instead of perceiving that it said more about me than cash ever could, since Neiman-Marcus has probably not dealt in cash since the days when each State issued its own currency, the assistant said: 'I'm sorry, sir, we only take our own charge card here.' I said I didn't have one. He said that would be fine, he'd issue me one right there. I explained that I was going back to England that night. He said that was fine too. I told him I didn't have my passport on me. He said that I wouldn't need any ID. I asked why not. He said, 'Because you have an American Express card.' I got the sweater, too.)

When they finally agree to accept one of the pieces of plastic you possess, the clerk will feed the magnetic strip through a small machine linked to a phone line. This is your credit check, which also automatically debits your card account. One computer sends a stream of electronic signals to another, and if it likes the signals it gets back, the padded Garfield sweatshirt is yours. In the old days the assistant had to pick up a phone and recite a series of numbers to some clearing centre thousands of miles away where they were checked by a real, live human being. I used to like the thought that the phone was linked to a bank of gossipy old ladies who would trade tit-bits. 'Ooh, it's that 4783-202-1787! He's been buying lingerie again, and not in his wife's size!'

If the electronic pulses are wrong, then your card is rejected. In an upmarket store, the clerk will murmur to you very discreetly, rather in the manner of a country solicitor explaining that a wealthy uncle in Australia has just died, leaving you nothing at all. If it is a store less solicitous of its customers' feelings, they will be more direct. At William Bell's discount establishment in Washington, my Visa card was spat out by the machine. Somehow the assistant managed to say, very loudly, 'Your-card-has-been-rejected-don't-take-it-up-with-me-take-it-up-with-your-issuing-bank' – all as a single syllable.

One alternative to the mall is the factory outlet. These are places where the big name brands can sell 'seconds', damaged goods and outdated lines to people who otherwise couldn't afford them. Some towns, such as Freeport, Maine, and Martinsburg, West Virginia, are now dominated by factory outlets. Millions of people stop each year to stock up on designer brandnames, so they end up looking like a walking menagerie, with the Ralph Lauren polo pony on their pocket and a Lacoste alligator on their breast, or else covered in lettering like a roll of credits: Calvin Klein, Liz Claiborne, YSL. In a place like Martinsburg it's actually quite hard to find any shop that isn't selling at a cut price; one suspects the news stand has to pretend that the local paper usually costs 35 cents in order to get people to pay a quarter for it.

Ralph Lauren is a good example of the Englandland style in America. This is doubly imitation Anglo, a replica not of the real thing, but of how Americans imagine the real thing to be, rather like those Olde Englishe Tavernes abroad which might be convincing except that they are insufficiently dirty, noisy and rude. Lauren's advertising shows impossibly handsome young men and women lounging around stately homes in their heather mixture tweeds and hard wearing woollies. What we know and they don't is that among British nobs, being well-dressed is thought to be a sign of the effete and foreign. Anyhow, real aristocrats never buy new clothes. If a suit was good enough for your great-grandfather, it's good enough for you.

Once a Californian friend of mine took me into a Lauren outlet and pointed admiringly at a garment unlike anything I had seen before. It was a sort of green cardigan with those leather buttons like old fashioned footballs, and it had beige suede facings on the front. 'That,' he declared, 'is something any English gentleman would be proud to wear.' 'That,' I was forced to reply, 'is something any English gentleman would regard as fit for wiping down a sweaty horse.'

One rule of thumb is that the less merchandise there is on view, the posher the store must be. In the wealthier areas of New York or Los Angeles you can see shops which will have, say, a total of a single sweater in the window, but since it costs 3,000 dollars, that's quite enough. Inside, the shelves are almost bare. If you have to ask to see it, you can't afford it. In Palm Beach, where even the fire hydrants are covered in chrome, nothing so

126

vulgar as a price tag ever disfigures the merchandise. Some shops in Rodeo Drive in Beverly Hills won't even let you in if you haven't established credit. At less glittering emporia, such as the K-Mart chain, it's the other way round. They won't let you out.

Food stores are among the glories of America. The most stupendous grocery I have ever seen was the Safeway in Page, Arizona. Page is a small town in the middle of the desert, surrounded by millions of acres of scrub and sand. But it also serves the dam on Lake Powell, so it gets a lot of visitors and a lot of people living there who have plenty of money because no one would work in Page unless they were well paid to do so.

Boris Yeltsin, the Soviet politician, says he cried when he entered a typical American supermarket. If he had seen the Page Safeway he would have been racked by such great sobs that his hosts would have had to use the Heimlich Manoeuvre on him. Cereal shelves the length of a football field. Ninety-seven different types of yoghurt. More French wines than you would expect in a French supermarket. Heaps of fresh seafood a thousand miles from the sea. Vast, dizzying towers of produce, cliffs of oranges, embankments of melons, escarpments of asparagus, all kept fresh and crisp in 110° temperatures by means of remoreseless air-conditioning and the application, at frequent intervals, of artificial dew.

All around the world people live in deserts, and they expect to adapt their lives accordingly. They live in tents so they can move easily to where the water is. They conserve food and liquids. They have a limited diet. America is the only country in the world where desert dewellers believe they have the right to live precisely as if they inhabited the centre of a large, temperate city.

To the foreigner's eye, most American supermarkets look much the same. There will be the same display of cardboard cereals, all labelled 'High in fibre', the same limitless selection of snacks, including Hawaiian hand-made super-thick lo-cholesterol potato chips and Twinkies, fizzy drinks shelving as long as a football pitch, and, at the check-out, bags of charcoal of a size which might be handy if your long-lost son had called to say he was on his way home, and the fatted calf was looking anxious.

The differences are slightly more subtle. You would not expect to find a lobster tank in West Memphis, Arkansas, which is a very poor town, though I suppose it's possible they have a place in the back where you can pick out your own raccoon. Instead you would find a meat counter stacked high with turkey gizzards, pigs' feet, and chitterlings. In West Memphis people are obliged to eat the parts of the pig which polite pigs don't care to talk about. I doubt if they shift a lot of sparkling spring water or Brie there, unlike Washington. A few years ago, during some obscure trade war, the United States threatened to ban imports of luxury foods from Europe. However, there was never the faintest chance that administration leaders would cause a deliberate shortage of bresola or pepper Boursin at the 'Social' Safeway in Wisconsin Avenue. There would have been mass starvation at Georgetown cocktail parties, and the business of government would have ground to a halt.

The core of the supermarket is the check-out, which is where your social position is established. At the top of the ladder you have a trolley which squeals under its load of beef tenderloins, fine wines, exotic lettuces in fluorescent colours, giant shrimps, and bread so nutty and crunchy and honest it tastes as if they had imported real Italian peasants' toenails to give it added texture. At the bottom, you pay with food stamps. Which magazine do you fling into the basket as you pass the racks at each check-out point? Is it *Vanity Fair* or *GQ*? Or the *National Enquirer*? It's not uncommon to see clearly well educated, even upper-class, people wait until the last possible moment before flicking a copy of *The Star* on to the moving belt, hoping that sleight of hand will prevent those behind them in line from noticing. But then who could resist a headline like 'Talking Bear Stole My Wife'? Or 'Hitler Still Alive: Evil Nazi Masterminded Invasion of the Falklands'?

There are no secrets in the check-out line. One American journalist made a tidy living going through Garbage of the Famous, deducing the small inner secrets of their lives from what they threw into their trash cans. He would have done much better following them to the check-out. Why the six pounds of eggplant? Or the two dozen cans of gourmet cat food? Given the special

128

'Lite' yoghurt and diet soda, are those six tubs of rich, full-fat ice-cream such a good idea? Once I watched a small drama as a yuppie couple bought one of those kits which tell you when to have intercourse for the maximum chance of conception. The check-out girl didn't know the price and had to ask, leaving the couple miserable and embarrassed. Were they really desperate for a child, or just so busy with their lives that they could not risk wasting even two minutes of their time on fruitless love-making?

Long check-out lines are one reason why Americans these days are so keen on shopless shopping, or mail order. Once we got back from a vacation to find at our front door a best-selling book, a pair of shoes and a bag of onions – not the detritus left by a squatter, but by the mailman. These days you can buy virtually anything in the US by post.

Food for example. Not milk, to be sure – you have to get that the old-fashioned way, by climbing into the car and driving to the nearest mart – but just about anything else. Slabs of smoked bacon. Prime Nebraska steaks, packed in dry ice. The 'Fruit of the Month' club sends crates of over-sized vegetation right to your home. You can even get a complete lobster dinner delivered to your door. Your friend sends you the (extremely expensive) gift voucher. Then, when you feel peckish, you phone up the company in Maine and they ship the live crustaceans, packed with seaweed in a special lobster steamer, overnight via the Federal Express headquarters in Memphis. Even if you lived in Maine yourself, the creatures would have to go via Memphis, though gourmets fear that jet lag does little for a lobster's tenderness.

Then there is the famous 'De-Luxe' fruitcake, from Corsicana, Texas. This sweetmeat, which would make good filler if they ever need to re-inter Jimmy Hoffa, is sent through the mail by film stars, to their friends all over the world, or so the makers claim. It does not have a shelf-life so much as a half-life, which in our case was just under a year, after which we realized there was still half left, and threw it out to make room for the next one.

Mail order used to be thought downmarket. Roseanne Barr, whose stand-up act was much funnier than her predictable sitcom, used to have a put-down line: 'Do you think I'd marry some guy who wore mail-order pants?' Some of it still is extremely tacky. We used to get catalogues from companies which sell 'Scripture tea bags' with a different inspirational text on each paper tag, tiny vacuum blackhead removers, jokey doormats marked 'Oh no, not you again!', a Galway crystal bottle with rubber teat, described as 'baby's first heirloom', 'willie warmers' in amusing animal shapes, and, I swear on a Scripture tea bag this is true, a device to toilet train your cat. It's a sort of seat, filled with various herbs cats are alleged to like, which you hook over the loo, optimistically.

Then there is the famous Frederick's of Hollywood saucy underwear catalogue. This is clothing for the kind of people who live in trailer parks, and for whom static cling is half the fun. We got the catalogue for four months, then they sent a stern little note saying that since we hadn't bought anything, they were going to stop. Naturally they don't want their mailing list clogged with the kind of people who like looking at pictures of gorgeous women with very little on. Well, actually, they're not so much gorgeous as buxom. They are the kind of women who have curves in places where other women go on to liquid diets in order not to have places at all.

By contrast, the Victoria's Secret lingerie catalogue is full of upmarket gorgeous women, though in a similar state of undress. They just bulge less. In a typical pose there is a young woman in a scanty silk chemise, wearing glasses and perusing what appears to be a rare first edition. The fancier catalogues these days are almost ludicrously snobbish: the models look as if they were relaxing at the Harvard Club, or on the deck of a yacht, or in the locker rooms at the polo club.

Others offer a different fantasy. Obtain the Eddie Bauer catalogue and you, an office worker, can picture yourself as a tough outdoorsman. Fantasy is quickly made reality. Phone the toll free number and the person at the other end greets you as if your call was the most wonderful thing that has happened to her all week. Within days, the fibre-glass socks and the quilted jacket stuffed with the down of two dozen geese are at your door. Carried away with an absurd self-image, I once bought a pair of 'hunter's mitts' from Eddie Bauer. They were handsome fleece-lined chamois mittens, normal in every way except that there was a flap opening at the top of the right-hand glove, to accommodate your trigger finger.

Quite the most wonderfully disgusting catalogue I've seen came from F. A. O. Schwarz, the country's poshest chain of toy stores. One year their Christmas catalogue contained a star present: for 180,000 dollars, your child starring in a cartoon film of his own story. Or, if you only love your child one-tenth as much, for 18,000 dollars you could buy 'the birthday party of a lifetime'. That's for fourteen children; a bigger thrash costs extra. It sounds fairly horrible: a limo from the airport in New York, rooms in a luxury hotel, and long hours spent browsing in the F. A. O. Schwarz toyshop on Fifth Avenue. Strictly for the child who has everything, including a sickening sense that someone else might have more.

More realistically, parents can pay a mere 14,500 dollars for a model Ferrari, which can run at 28 m.p.h., or a miserable 2,500 dollars for a toy Mercedes, top speed a sluggish 13 m.p.h. The same price secures a child's mink coat, which can be 'tossed over a pair of jeans' or worn with 'velvet and pearls, for dining à deux with Dad'.

Schwarz also sells a British-made rocking horse, carved in Kent from American walnut. The makers have shown their commitment to the export trade by providing the kind of resonant drivel people seem to expect when writing a cheque for a large sum, in this case 4,500 dollars. 'To honour this precious resource they have pledged to plant a tree for every horse they make ... each will arrive with a note (sealed, time-capsule like, in the belly) that expresses the feelings and thoughts of the artisan who carved it.' One has this vision of the horse cracking open a hundred years from now, and a twinkle-eyed old lady reading the innermost feelings of the Kentish craftsman who carved it a century ago and so cast a special magic over her childhood: 'Blimey, I could murder a cup of tea.'

My favourite catalogue was from Lands' End, partly because it's the most honest. It offers clothes for the Sixties generation who have just about come to terms with growing up. The catalogue is

like a jolly magazine, with articles about how their adventurous buyers set off for Tibet to find yak wool for those hard-wearing yet easy-press pants which are as much at home in the office as they are on the beach. The models have terrific figures and great smiles, but they look normal, and they're doing normal kinds of things, such as playing with the kids or barbecuing a bunch of burgers. You yearn to join them, share their jokes, toss the football with them, which no doubt is why Lands' End sells around 300 million dollars' worth of clothes each year – though paradoxically the recent Sixties revival has made times somewhat harder for the company. It's tougher selling clothes to people who, having decided it's time to grow up, figure that they do want that tie-dyed sweater in psychedelic colours, after all.

SEVEN

On the Road Again

Americans adore to travel, but are nervous about leaving home. The result is that businesses which cater to travellers try to be as identical as they possibly can. The plan is that you should be able to wake up in Tampa, Dallas or Tuscaloosa, and have no immediate means of knowing the difference. Ideally, having flipped on the TV from the bedside console, you cannot be sure where you are until Willard Scott, the wacky weatherman on the popular NBC *Today* show finishes his shtick about the multitudinous attractions of Erie, Pennsylvania, where he is currently wearing a hat topped with elk's antlers, surrounded by members of a bake club, and adds: 'Here's what's happening in your world, even as we speak.' Some nonentity in a plaid sports coat, weatherman for the local station then has approximately five seconds to say: 'Looks like rain all day here' while you have the same time to glimpse the map behind him. 'Ah, yes, Wheeling!' you cry. Or Duluth, or Houston, or Buffalo. No hint of your location is to be found in the room. A friend of mine, related to the British aristocracy, once stayed at the Travelodge in Des Moines, Iowa, and found a print of his family home in Northumberland on the wall.

Moving at great speed across the continent, while actually staying in the same place, is somehow very comforting and familiar. This is how you might cross America using, say, the Holiday Inn chain. First you call their toll-free phone number and make a reservation for your first stop. You have to give them a credit card number. If you don't turn up, and haven't cancelled before six o'clock, you get to pay anyway. On the other hand, the room is held for you all night. This means that you are 50 dollars in the red, and the poor commercial traveller who turned up at seven has to sleep in his car.

Off you go. The air-conditioning keeps the ambient temperature the same wherever you happen to be. The road signs on the freeway are an identical white and green. Radio stations come and go, but they're all much the same. 'Yes, God asks only that you pay him a Life Premium, friends, and you'll be fully insured by the Lord. A woman in Odessa, Texas, sent a Life Premium of a hundred dollars right here to this ministry, and the very next day she heard the blessed news that her son had been cured of cancer. Friends, the Lord never rips you off!'

Top 40 stations are playing Paula Abdul. Golden Oldie stations have the Grateful Dead. If you're lucky, the country station might play Hank Williams's great hit 'My Son Calls Another Man Daddy'. Or my all-time favourite C & W title: 'You're the Reason Our Kids Are Ugly'.

If you're even luckier, you might get National Public Radio, usually confined to an unwanted slot near the bottom of the FM band. 'The President has been shot dead, and the Vice-President has been sworn in. But first, here's Charles McDavitt with some amusing advice on how to stay friends with your cat.' At least NPR is a real person talking to you, not some demented maniac who sounds as if he would, were he not in a studio, be running around outside with a meat cleaver. Halfway across Nebraska, a hundred miles from anywhere, hearing the calm voice of NPR can be as delightful as spotting an old, dear friend at a particularly dreary party.

Outside, the scenery changes unnervingly, but who cares? In front of you, the road stretches ahead, pulling you relentlessly along, never allowing you to halt. Americans are always writing books about travelling around the country, such as *On the Road* and *Blue Highways*, but Kerouac and William Least Heat Moon got it wrong. They kept stopping to meet people. Why? That's not what the super-highways are for. You'll never get any place if you stop to chat, or look at things.

You set imaginary goals, such as 'Spokane', just 180 miles ahead. For three hours your whole being is suffused with the

135

necessity of reaching Spokane. Suddenly you're there, but really you're not there at all. The road rushes along an overpass and you glide over the rush hour at 60 m.p.h. Below you are traffic jams, churches, shops, schoolchildren being bussed back home, but they might as well be on the planet Neptune. Already the signs are beckoning you onward to Coeur d'Alene, Missoula, Butte, Billings and Bozeman.

In the Holiday Inn the Holidex computer has done its work, and you're soon installed in your room. It has a big comfy bed, a thick fluffy carpet, a series of little bottles of shampoo and conditioner, plus a plastic shower cap and a generous selection of plastic cups. On top of the TV is a leaflet which informs you that for an extra $5.95, later that night you can watch a pornographic movie with the dirty bits taken out. Another leaflet enjoins you to try the 'Last Round-Up Lounge' where cocktails and hors d'oeuvres are served every night in an authentic Western atmosphere, with live entertainment from a group with a faintly surrealist name: 'Cinnamon', perhaps, or 'It's a Pleasure' or 'Those Heggarty Boys'. Or there might be a pianist, tinkling out 'Feelings'.

These lounges are important, and should not be missed. Their aim is to offer the character of the surrounding area without your having to leave the Holiday Inn. There are recently built hotels in New Orleans where the lounges provide the raffish excitement of that city's famous French Quarter – even though the real French Quarter is only half a mile away.

Your room is now your home for the next week or so. You might imagine that you are going to be four hundred miles away the next night and so, in one sense, you will be. But you'll still be in the same room. The same furniture, the same pots of shampoo, the same films on the cable TV. In the hallway is the same Coke machine, the same ice dispenser, and in the elevator the same injunction to enjoy a delicious steak, char-grilled to perfection, and served with your choice of fries or baked potato, including a trip to our bountiful salad bar!

It's all very reassuring. Even on the fabulous American superhighways driving is wearisome. After a day behind the wheel, the last thing you want to do is to start absorbing a new culture. You want to absorb a large drink instead, followed by a slow shower. A branding iron and a saddle stuck up on the bar wall represent quite enough local colour for one night, thank you very much. In a Holiday Inn, or a Ramada, or a Days Inn, or any other chain, everything is as cosy and familiar as your own home. Americans have taken Einstein's theory to its logical conclusion: the faster you travel, the less you age and the more things stay the same.

The following day (after your breakfast of two slices crispy bacon, eggs over easy, and hash browns, served with toast and Smuckers grape jelly, slogan: 'With a name like Smuckers, it's got to be good'. Well, up to a point) you need to make a reservation for the next Holiday Inn. The desk clerk is delighted to help, and within minutes the computer has chatted out details of your booking. It's as if you were towing a gigantic motor home behind you, with the front desk staff, the chambermaids, the bar girls in their slit skirts and the poster for half-price beer during Monday Night Football all trundling with you to the next destination.

Back on the highway, and the businesses whizzing past are all part of the conspiracy to keep you on the road. 'Stop here. We won't keep you long', they promise. Fifty-foot signs proclaim 'Gas 'n' Go', 'This Stop: Fast Food', 'Ten-Minute Lube'. 'Drive Thru' Burgers', says another, pledging that you won't need to cut the engine, and can eat your hamburger on the move, one-handed, as the road relentlessly speeds you forward. A friend of mine swears he saw: 'One Stop: Eat n' 'Gas'.

Sometimes people miss the point. Once we saw a sign advertising the 'Tarry-a-While Motel'. Tarry? Here? No, thank you, we have to be on our way to the next Holiday Inn.

There's a splendid series of guides called *The Interstate Gourmet* which tells you how you can find delicious food within a few miles of the freeways. We tried it several times and had excellent meals even in New Jersey, where the turnpike service areas are to fine dining what the Black Hole of Calcutta was to the Great Outdoors. On the other hand, the guide also misses the point. Nobody on the freeways wants to leave. They are in their own enclosed world, a womb 2,500 miles long. Why find your way out, why leave the asphalt ribbon and risk getting lost on roads which

137

might not even be labelled, and sit in restaurants where it can take as long as half an hour to eat?

And you can find everything near the freeway. On I-64 near St Louis, you can buy drugs on the hard shoulder. On I-95 just north of Miami, hoodlums sometimes stage fake accidents to stop drivers, who can then be mugged without even leaving the comfort of their own cars.

Some years ago Lady Bird Johnson persuaded Congress to ban advertising on Interstate highways, in the interests of beauty and road safety, which is pretty ridiculous since in some places, such as New Jersey, hoardings would do much to improve the view, especially if they were 100 feet high. A few manage to get near the road. In Wisconsin I passed a poster which declared, 'Next exit – Cheese!' They produce a lot of cheese in Wisconsin, most of it named after cheese producing areas of Europe, on the same principle as Romanian Burgundy.

The road itself is so magnetic that you don't actually need a lot going on in the brain to make the time pass by. I find that an Easy Listening station which plays ten Barry Manilow hits in a row is usually sufficient mental stimulation. But if you need more, you can always spot the licence plates of your fellow drivers. Each State has its own distinctive plates, and many of them carry a slogan boosting its virtues. 'Illinois – Land of Lincoln' or 'Alabama – Heart of Dixie'. Minnesota claims 'Ten Thousand Lakes', West Virginia is 'Wild, Wonderful', Tennessee 'The Volunteer State', and so forth. Some are feeble puns: 'Utah: Greatest Snow on Earth' or 'Washington DC: A Capital City'. Some are historical, such as South Carolina's 'First in Flight', which celebrates the Wright Brothers, and New Hampshire's 'Live Free Or Die' which commemorates the fact that until recently the inhabitants of the State gave the impression that the reason they were armed to the teeth was because they were expecting the Redcoats any moment, which they probably still are, except that they have been infiltrated instead by Bostonians, who dislike the British for quite different reasons.

Some of the plates are absurd, such as 'New Jersey – The Garden State'. Some tempt fortune, such as 'You've Got A Friend

In Pennsylvania', which you only ever notice when some complete asshole from Pittsburg has just cut in front of you. Some are curiously flat, such as 'Oklahoma Is OK'. Try saying it with a short pause before the 'OK'. The most desperate was Idaho's. I felt sorry for the inhabitants. Imagine you're some fast-track accountant in Boise, and you've just bought your first Porsche. You zoom south to Vegas with a platinum-haired bimbette beside you, but everywhere you park people read your plates – 'Famous Potatoes' – and realize that beneath it all you're just another dumb hick. They've changed it now.

You could pass the time inventing your own honest slogans. Illinois could become 'Land of Capone'. Florida would be 'A Great Place To Die'. Noël Coward fans would appreciate 'Very Flat, Kansas'. Iowa could claim 'Better Than Nebraska' and Nebraska itself, home of Strategic Air Command, could be 'First Target State'. California might squeeze on: 'You Don't Have To Be Mad To Live Here, But It Helps'. Colorado, which is now home to innumerable mystical sects, could promote: 'You Only Live Twice'. Texas would be 'Execution State.'

Every State has an official State flower, animal and so on, all actually voted on by its legislature. Why not spend a moment figuring out the official State cars? Here are a few suggestions to get you started:

Connecticut: Volvo
Virgina: horse box
Florida: Lincoln Town Car with leather seating ('the mobile
    coffin')
North Dakota: Oldsmobile, with space for cow in back
New York: black stretch limo with TV and phone
California: ditto, only pink, with working Jacuzzi
Arizona: U-Haul rental van (slogan: 'Adventure in Moving')
Texas: pick-up truck with gun rack
New Hampshire: Jaguar with gun rack
West Virginia: 15-year-old lime green Plymouth, no wheels

If you are unlucky you might not have time to cross the country by road, and may be obliged to take a plane. Americans complain a lot about air travel, rather in the way that British people moan about British Rail, though with less reason. I think the Americans are, by and large, wrong. I love going by plane. Once I got a cheap upgrade to first class on a United Airlines flight from Chicago to Vancouver. There weren't many people in the cabin, but one of them was Dolly Parton, so that was a good start. Then the cabin staff appeared with fresh lobster and champagne. Then they made us a Caesar salad, right there on the spot. Then they wheeled on a whole prime rib of roast beef. Then they invited us to devise our own desserts from various flavours of ice-cream, fresh fruits, nuts, fudge and chocolate sauce. All washed down with wonderful wines. The flight alone would have justified the triumph of capitalism. (Miss Parton also gave me a devastating smile. She is the smallest fully grown person I have ever seen. Her famous bosom is, in fact, normal size; it just looks huge on that minuscule frame.)

Usually you're in the back with the rest of the cattle. But even here there are compensations, though they don't come in the form of the meal, which is likely to be bizarre, as if assembled by an anorexic bohemian, such as a frozen croissant and a thin mint. You are, of course, a member of all the frequent flier mileage schemes, so that every cramped minute that passes you are clocking up more points towards that vacation you're planning, which can't be in Hawaii, since free travel there has been booked up until well into the next millennium, though there are still seats to Detroit.

During most of 1988, the airlines locked themselves into a frequent flier war. They offered triple mileage points to members who had signed up before the end of March. This was also election year, a time when journalists must travel a lot. Usually when you meet colleagues during elections you chat about the candidates, or the polls, or the latest scandal. In 1988 conversations went like this:

You: How did you get here?

Your colleague: Oh, on United. I flew to Denver, picked up a connection to Anchorage, managed to get standby to San Francisco, and caught the red-eye to Miami.

You: But you started from Miami.

Colleague: Yeah, I'm hoping to take the family to Sydney this year. First class.

One man I knew, an Englishman, became obsessional about his frequent flier miles. He went everywhere on Pan Am. One spring and early summer, he had to cross the Atlantic ten times. He had enough miles tó take himself and his girlfriend anywhere he wanted on earth. But he couldn't face getting on another plane. So he drove to the beach instead. It's clear by now that many people are collecting their frequent flier miles purely for the pleasure of owning them, like Michael Milken makes money just to see the numbers growing in their columns. Some cannot bear to spend what they have accumulated. They are the Silas Marners of the business travel world. The psychological blow of dropping from 100,000 miles in your account to a miserable 50 would be too great and, apart from anything else, would ruin the vacation.

On board, the airlines have developed their own language, which bears some distant resemblance to English. It obeys few rules of grammar, or even sense, but is meant to soothe and comfort, and distract your attention from (a) the fact that you can see there are eighteen planes ahead of you for take-off, and (b) you are about to be given a supper of reconstituted in-flight magazines, sometimes referred to in this curious pidgin as 'lasagne'. There's a curious sing-song delivery too, which diverts attention from the meaning. They stress the words which don't matter: 'and', 'with', 'would'.

'Ladies and gentlemen, this *is* Flight 913 *with* service to Denver and continuing service *to* San Diego. If neither of these two cities feature in your travel plans today, now would be a good time·to deplane.'

What would they do if someone demanded to know if it was the very finest time to deplane, and insisted on waiting on board a while longer to see if a better psychological moment arrived? Or do they just mean that it's a good time compared to when the plane has reached 25,000 feet? What they can't say is, 'You're on the wrong plane, get off now', because that would shatter the mood of genteel, nervous courtesy which has been so painstakingly built up.

On United flights they let you listen on the earphones to the conversations between air traffic control and the flight deck. These had a clipped jocularity, the easy patter of professionals who are short of time but want to be established as regular guys, at ease with themselves and their skill. (A 'heavy' is jargon for any widebodied plane.) 'All righty, United 379, see that Delta heavy there? I want you to git your nose right up behind his rear end for me . . . Okay, United 379, you're ready to roll . . .' Then United planes started dropping out of the sky with alarming frequency, and for a while they stopped it, so instead you had to listen on the regular sound system to Bob Newhart's 'Driving Instructor' sketch for the 674th time in your life.

Animal societies forced to live very close together develop elaborate codes of conduct designed to make their existence bearable. Airline passengers do the same. Remember to get a pee before the drinks come round, so the person next to you doesn't get Diet Coke on his only clean shirt when you try to climb past him. Don't embarrass your neighbour by screaming with rage when they announce that, owing to equipment problems, you won't actually be taking off for Atlanta for at least one hour, but you mustn't leave the plane because they may need to leave at a moment's notice. Americans don't like scenes, unlike the British who quite enjoy them. Don't start a conversation if the person next to you is reading (with the exception of the in-flight magazine, since the article on 'Dayton – A City Looks to the Future' is so boring that in laboratory tests, rats who were read the first three paragraphs began to eat themselves.)

As a rule, the person next to you will be a tedious businessman who spends the whole trip anxiously scanning a computer print-out. For light relief, he may go to the magazine rack, returning with a copy of *Black Enterprise*, which is the only publication left, the eighteen-week-old copies of *Sports Illustrated* having all been snaffled. Do not make the mistake of engaging him in conversation. He may turn out to be an Amway salesman. Amway is the biggest pyramid selling operation in the US, and since the people who work for it can only get rich by enrolling even more people who pay commissions to them, and who enrol other people in turn, the manner tends to be distinctly evangelical, as if a missionary were working on a commission system. Amway predicates a version of America in which the entire population earns its money by selling things to everybody else, like Lewis Carroll's island where the inhabitants scratch a living by taking in each other's washing.

I once sat next to such a person. I realized as we were flying over West Virginia that he was an Amway salesman – and we weren't going to touch down until Salt Lake City. After twenty minutes of his graphs and flow charts and expositions on how I might become rich by selling handyman equipment to my nearest and dearest I could cheerily have thrown myself out of the plane. As it was my fate was worse: hours pretending to read 'Cleveland – City on the Go' and 'San Antonio – Where History Meets Enterprise' in the in-flight magazine. I realized with relief that those long advertisements written in story form ('I guess, like a lot of people, I laughed when a friend told me I needed a hand-held photocopier. You would too. But have you ever tried getting the office Xerox into your carry-on bag? . . . these sunglasses with their magenta lenses will block 90 per cent of deadly gamma rays . . .') were prepared entirely for people who find themselves sitting next to Amway salesmen.

Usually there is in the area where you wait for your plane at least one extremely attractive person of the opposite sex. When you finally get on the plane, he or she will not be sitting next to you. You will be next to that very fat man who has brought two immense bags with him which you would think the airline would refuse to accept in the hold but by some crass oversight have been allowed in the cabin. He may also be an Amway salesman.

American trains are fabulously romantic, or at least they used to be. Those wonderful railroad names: the 'Union Pacific', the 'Atchison, Topeka & Santa Fe', the 'Burlington and Northern'. Once I saw a mile-long procession of freight cars winding across Wyoming, with several diesels at the front marked, in modernistic

143

print, 'Rock Island Railroad'. The Rock Island Line still exists, no longer carrying passengers, but still hauling pig iron, just like in the song. (Though Rock Island itself, a river town in Illinois, is somewhere you probably don't wish to visit.)

At some point, Amtrak, the national semi-public rail network, must have decided that the romance of the railroad was dead. Far more people took the plane these days, and this was presumably because they preferred travelling on planes. Therefore, they made the experience of sitting on a train as close as possible to that available in the air. What never seems to have crossed their minds is that people take the plane because it's quicker, and that if they choose to spend the extra time on a train, they expect it to be more spacious, more relaxed and comfortable.

Amtrak introduced smaller, higher windows, so that only a professional footballer could sit up enough to enjoy the passing panorama. They started to serve microwaved ready-meals in the restaurant, which was re-named the 'Amcafé'. They fitted airline-style seats (admittedly somewhat wider) with nowhere to rest your head. And they even slotted an in-flight magazine into the seat in front of you. Then they wondered why people weren't flooding back to the railroads.

It's all very well sitting on a train with some marvellous name redolent of the Golden Age of rail travel: 'The City of New Orleans' or 'The Empire Builder', but not if it ought to be renamed 'The Back of a 727'. The trains still have that marvellous, mournful long whistle, like Bigfoot calling for his mate, and the conductors do cry 'All Ab-o-o-o-ard' before the train leaves, but it's hard to capture the romance of the Chattanooga Choo-Choo (which no longer runs; Chattanooga, Tennessee, has no passenger rail service) while you sit in just another fuselage.

The Club Car is no longer a mobile lounge with liveried waiters bringing cocktails to your table. The seats are slighty wider, but your drink and microwaved beef stew have to perch on the fold-down tray in the back of the seat in front. The crucial scene in *Double Indemnity*, where Fred McMurray chats to a fellow passenger before throwing himself off the little patio at the back of the train, could not occur today.

What's nice is that the Amtrak staff are marvellously fussy. As soon as you arrive on the train they clip to the rack a little ticket with your destination on it (reduced to a three-letter code, like the airlines have, so that Baltimore is BAL and Washington WAS; they really have become fixated on the idea that we like everything about air travel, and need to be constantly reminded of it). Then for the whole of your trip they will anxiously patrol the train making sure that everyone has been alerted well in advance that very soon – within an hour perhaps – their destination will have been reached. At the same time announcements are constantly made over the public address system. For you to miss a station you would need to be in a coma, and even then they would know to wheel you off. It often struck me that Amtrak could save much trouble by adopting the European system of putting the name of the station somewhere visible on the platform, though of course this would deprive an awful lot of people of their jobs.

EIGHT

The Permanent Hall of Fame

Drive into any American small town and there, perhaps outside a gas station or the 'Ruby's Eat' Café, you are likely to see one of those big illuminated signs where you can slide in lettering to spell different messages. 'Congratulations, Bruce Striebster, Fosterville Fighting Firecats Player of the Week. Way To Go, Bruce!' it says, or something equally hortatory. You can deduce from this that the Fighting Firecats are the local high-school football team, and that in the previous week Bruce Striebster scored a touchdown, or made a perfect thirty-yard pass, or by his dogged determination in defence prevented a humiliating defeat by the Waukasheekah Wolverines from becoming a massacre.

The chances are that this will be the peak of Bruce's sporting glory. His hopes of playing football at college are, by the law of averages, very slight, and the possibility of his becoming a professional virtually non-existent, if only because he is a mere 6 foot 3 inches tall and weighs but 225 pounds. (In a bar on Cape Cod I once met a professional footballer, who played for the New England Patriots. He was the largest and tallest human being I have ever encountered. You had to bellow up at him. It was like trying to hold a conversation with the Goodyear blimp.) However, even if he leaves home and works in Alaska for twenty-five years, Bruce will be able to return to Fosterville one day and someone will say: 'Bruce Striebster? That name sure rings a bell. Weren't you Firecats' Player of the Week back aways?'

Countries which regard sport as being of overwhelming importance have a problem. In order to discover the finest athletes, they need to have an enormous number of people training, playing and working out – even though the vast majority know they will never get remotely near the top. To find one Joe Montana, you need ten thousand Bruce Striebsters not only dreaming that they might be quarterback for the San Francisco 49'ers, but actually prepared to risk a major hernia in pursuit of the fantasy. In East Germany they were able to find the best athletes by holding out the promise of cars, holidays and the chance of living in a flat which didn't have seven close relatives sharing it. In America young people generally have these privileges already, so they must be offered something even more beguiling, in this case celebrity. The system works at all levels. Joe Namath and Mickey Mantle are nationally famous and can earn huge sums of money lending their names to restaurants or advertising aftershave, but if Bruce Striebster scores the winning touchdown in a close-fought game against a local school, well then he's as famous in Fosterville as William 'The Refrigerator' Perry is.

A small high school in a town called Milan, Indiana (it's pronounced 'My-lan') once won the State basketball championship against a much bigger and better-known school. The man who threw the winning basket is celebrated not only in Milan but around the country. He is still frequently interviewed on the radio and asked to relive his emotions at the time. No sporting event is too obscure to shine its glory upon the participants. Which is also why young men and women are prepared to play their hearts out for a team most of us will never hear of.

I once went to lecture at the Tuscaloosa campus of the University of Alabama. I arrived on a Sunday to discover that the previous day the University had defeated their arch-rivals Auburn in the final moments of the game. Nobody wanted to talk about anything else. I was introduced to elderly academics who, in any European country, would have been hard put to converse about any more than two topics – their own speciality and, if pressed, the weather. At Tuscaloosa every conversation began: 'Whew, how 'bout that game there! How *about* it!' I met a couple in their nineties who were able to provide a comparison with numerous other similarly exciting games, going back beyond World War Two. In a class I taught, I mentioned the game, and the students, until then quiet and docile, began cheering wildly. One or two launched into the school chant and the girls waved mock pom-poms, as if they were cheerleaders. The dean of the faculty drove a nifty customized van with tinted windows, the whole vehicle painted in the team colours.

Sport is followed at whatever level it can be found. If you live in Los Angeles, you can support two major league baseball teams, two top-class football teams, the best basketball team in the world, and an ice hockey team which includes the Canadian Wayne Gretsky, who is thought to be the most expensive player ever purchased anywhere in the history of sport. In Paraquat, South Carolina, there is less choice. But if the Paraquat Junior High soccer team, consisting of an indeterminate number of small boys and/or girls chasing a ball twice the size of their heads round a soggy and unkempt patch of turf is all you have to support, support it you will. Quite likely there's a stadium, and cheerleaders. There are certainly tailgate picnicking parties, and parents who, when their offspring misses an open goal, react with the same calm they might display if they discovered a cache of cocaine in his teddy bear.

And if young Jason scores three times in the historic defeat of nearby Porringer, SC, then he will probably be inscribed in the Paraquat Junior High Sports Hall of Fame, to receive the plaudits of the school when, thirty years later, he returns as a balding fast-food franchise owner whose idea of athletic endeavour is raising the recliner in order to aim the remote control more accurately at the TV.

(It must be said that, while soccer is played at most American schools, it is not taken seriously as a sport. To most Americans it is a game for (a) hysterical Latins, (b) British hooligans, and (c) schoolchildren. American sports are like Australian fauna; having evolved in isolation, they have become different from anything else on the planet. One of the Darwinian ways they have adapted to survive is the imposition of lengthy breaks into which TV commercials can be inserted. At prominent football games, there is even an official wearing day-glo orange gloves whose job it is to tell the referee when the ads are over. Soccer has not acquired this protective device. When the 1986 World Cup was shown on American TV, to tiny audiences, the sponsor, the brewers Anheuser-Busch, used two techniques to get around the problem: they put a red 'collar' with the word 'Budweiser' on it around the frame, thus reducing each player to the size of three dots from the cathode ray tube, or sometimes just interrupted the play, often at the point where a goal was about to be scored, so that the commentator would have to say something along the lines of 'We welcome you back here to World Cup soccer with the news that Diego Maradona of Argentina has just scored what's already being called here the finest goal in World Cup history. We'll be showing you a replay of that goal just as soon as we can. Stay with us.' That is another reason why soccer will never catch on as a grown man's game in the US.)

American football is related to rugby in the way that we are related to the higher primates. The common ancestry is inescapable but the differences are impressive. The game has been called a paradigm of American life, being random violence interrupted by committee meetings. These meetings occupy roughly two-thirds of the time spent on the game. When the first American exhibition game was played at Wembley Stadium in London the fans, who had been used only to the edited highlights on British TV, began to chant, 'Boring, boring', reducing one American commentator to fury. 'Boring?' he screamed. 'From the people who invented *cricket*?'

In Europe we tend to sense that the rules of a game are handed down on tablets of stone. We change them as reluctantly as the Americans change their Constitution. In the States, however, the rules are fluid. Originally rugby was taught to the players of Harvard in 1874, by the Canadians of McGill University, Montreal. They began changing the rules from day one. It's as if wallabies had evolved from unicellular organisms in less than a century. Even now, several important changes are made each season. Most American fans cannot keep up with these, and referees and commentators become like rabbis who have mastered the Talmud; their arcane knowledge makes them into a form of priesthood. Whereas an English fan might shout, 'Get some glasses, ref!' an American would think it more fruitful to yell,

'Why doncha look at the rules, page 438, section IV, sub-section (d), paragraph (iii), ref!' Not that they do, because they are as baffled as everyone else.

American football is a wonderful spectacle. Go to an English game and you see mud-covered players performing in front of mud-coloured stands in a sea of mud. In America the stadium is a riot of colours, none of which is found in nature. Electric blues. Key-lime pie greens. Aquamarine from Zsa Zsa Gabor's bathroom. Tangerine from the side of a California police prowl car. That's just the players' uniforms. Every time the two teams get into the scrimmage, it creates the kind of colour combo which caused Liberace's decorator to wake up screaming.

Occasionally I would be able to go to a Washington Redskins game, which was considerable good fortune, since every one has been sold out since the year 1968. I was taken by our neighbour, who had season tickets. These are inherited and passed on through the family line. So to be invited to use one was on a par with the Duke of Devonshire asking if you would like to borrow his title for the weekend. We trotted along with two enormous leather shopping bags, from one of which my host pulled several bottles of soda, a set of tumblers and a bucket of ice, plus a carton of delicacies from a nearby gourmet grocery. From the other he dug out three pairs of binoculars, three of those radios you wear on your head with the receivers in the earpiece so that we could hear the commentary, and a portable, battery-powered television in order to watch the action replays. Thus equipped, with food and drink at our elbows, we were able to duplicate precisely the experience of watching the game at home on TV. We were not untypical. Many people around us were similarly kitted. (The Skyboxes at the Astrodome in Houston are so high up that their inhabitants are obliged to watch the game on TV because they can barely see the pitch.)

For us, the only difference was that during the commercial breaks, while the folks at home had to watch ads for cars and beer, we could train our binoculars on the lovely Redskinettes, whose apparently genuine ecstasy at every successful move made by the home team only served to boost the erotic charge they already radiated at approximately one million lumens. For many American males the notion of being a successful football player and so getting to bed a heavy-breasted blonde with a short skirt, pony-tail and the team's initial on her spandex bustier is the final sexual fantasy. And it actually happens for many young men, all around the country, thousands of times a season. In the United States the line between fantasy and reality has always been satisfyingly blurred.

In Washington, the apotheosis of real life and sport being intertwined occurs in the owner's box in RFK Stadium. For any team, the owner's box is the Ark of the Covenant, but at Cincinatti or Denver, the people who sit there are generally celebrities only in Cincinatti or Denver. In Washington they are nationally, sometimes internationally, famous. Turn your gaze from the Redskinettes and run your binoculars along the front row of the owner's box. Isn't that James Baker, the Secretary of State? And Senator Laxalt, Ronald Reagan's dearest friend in politics? And Lawrence Tisch, the owner of CBS, together with two of his stars, Dan Rather and Lesley Stahl, both of whom exist in the thinnest stratosphere of broadcasting fame? I once watched a game from the owners' box, along with Mr Neil Kinnock, the British Labour Party leader, who was visiting Washington and wanted to see the Redskins play. This was before Kinnock became famous in America for having written part of a speech which Joe Biden stole, thus ending his own presidential campaign. Even so, it was celebrity overkill in there. As stewardesses constantly passed between the rows of seats, making sure that nobody's glass was empty for longer than three seconds and bringing in fresh supplies of giant shrimp, the air was loud with people saying: 'Mr Kinnock? I'd like to have you meet Ted Koppel of the *Nightline* show.' 'Did you meet Senator Muskie, Mr Kinnock? I know you two fellows are going to have plenty to talk about.' Kinnock had to leave the game before the finish, in order to meet the then Democratic front runner Gary Hart. This was a genuine appointment, but in American terms it would have been a dazzling piece of one-upmanship. To leave the owner's box! And for someone even more famous than those left in it! For these celebrities, like

151

Caesar, the main point of going to the Games is to be on show to the loyal populace.

Football may, these days, be the most popular spectator sport in the US, but unlike baseball it is not thought to represent the very core of the American being. Most Americans are convinced that baseball sprang from their country's unique genius, or was at least invented in New York State by a man called Abner Doubleday. They are mistaken. One of the most effective conversation stoppers I know for dealing with a baseball bore was to inform him that the game is mentioned (as 'base ball') in the first chapter of *Northanger Abbey*. And that, under the name of 'rounders', it is played in British girls' schools, though for the most part without the whiff of sexual scandal which always seems to surround professional baseball. The late Babe Ruth, perhaps the finest player ever, was in the habit of smoking a cigar every time he made love to a woman. One morning a colleague found seven butts in the living-room of the suite they shared. What the Immortal Jane would have made of that, it is hard to know. These days it is fashionable for the better players to have lavish semi-public affairs, find themselves betrayed by the jilted mistress, and then appear, sobbing, on Barbara Walters's show, America's secular equivalent of the confessional box. One of these, Wade Boggs, had been turned upon by his former lover, a Miss Margo Adams, who attempted to sue him for 12 million dollars. Baseball fans tend to be obsessed with statistics, and part of her case was that while she was with him, he had a batting average of .341, but while his wife was in the stands, this was reduced to .221. One has this vision of Miss Adams arriving at the hotel, her bag containing exotic underwear and a laptop computer to work out how many times her lover had scored.

In spite of these diversions, the game is seen to be the very key to America, at least by many baseball writers, who greet each new season with lyrical essays about The Game, Humanity and the Soul of the United States. One of the best-known writers, Thomas Boswell, wrote a book called *How Life Imitates the World Series*, the World Series being, in spite of its name, the purely North American championship. He was only half joking.

153

Another celebrated writer is Roger Angell of the *New Yorker*, who writes at quite incredible length. Angell likes to take a metaphor and stretch it till it cries for mercy. No ball is safe; almost every one is described in pitiless detail. After a few pages of this you want to say, 'Look, Mr Angell, I'm a busy man. Wouldn't it be a whole lot quicker if I just flew to Seattle and watched the game myself?'

No one would dream of writing at such length about football, or hockey, or come to that, the future of East-West relations. They feel permitted to do it because baseball is seen as an analogy for anything you want it to be. It is no mere game; it is the *Zeitgeist*, or perhaps even the eternal human condition.

For an American male to play at any sport is a means of reaffirming his sense of being American – it is, perhaps, the masculine equivalent of shopping. But baseball carries more of these overtones than any other game. There is hardly a garage in the country which doesn't contain a Louisville Slugger brand bat and a couple of lovingly worn-down gloves (or rather, leather buckets with finger holes, which fielders wear on one hand, and which make catching the ball so easy that to miss one is to be guilty of the feared 'error', an official statistical judgement which goes down on a player's record, and which, unlike drunk driving offences, cannot be extirpated by time. In 1986 Bill Buckner of the Boston Red Sox committed, at a critical moment of the World Series, what came to be called 'The Error of the Century' when he let the ball roll between his legs. This led to the joke: 'What do Bill Buckner and Michael Jackson have in common?' 'They both wear a glove, for no apparent reason.' That mistake will be attached to Buckner's name for the remainder of his days. He could win the World Series single-handed, hitting eight home runs in a single game, or could invent a cure for AIDS, but the headline on his obituary would still read: 'Bill Buckner: Committed Error of the Century'.)

Taking a bat, a ball and a couple of mitts out into the yard isn't a rite of passage for American males; it's a continuing part of their lives, a means of asserting their continued commitment to being among the guys. Go into a New York lawyers' office where young men in power ties and mohair suits are busy making reservations at the Quilted Giraffe (and two hundred grand a year). On the noticeboard, set upon the mahogany panelling, will be that week's softball roster for the big game against Matheson, Shickley & Gruber. (Softball is baseball played with, naturally, a softer ball. It's shorter too, and there is significantly less chance that if a ball hits you, it will separate the twin hemispheres of your brain.)

You can see these games in any park in any big city every summer evening. The richer the people playing and the more sedentary their lives, the more hot-shot 'hubba hubba' fighting 'guy' talk there will be. Part of the satisfaction depends on pretending that the result is important. It's these people's way of saying, 'Look, I may be disgustingly rich, I may drive a BMW and vacation at a golf resort in the Caribbean, but, hey, really I'm still the same. I'm still that freckle-faced kid who dreamed one day he'd play at Yankee Stadium!' Horseshit, of course, but necessary horseshit.

A professional game is enormous fun to watch. One reason is that American fans are overwhelmingly better behaved than those on the other side of the Atlantic. For example, the usher who guides you to your place is quite likely to wipe off the seat before you sit on it, behaviour which at a British soccer stadium would be thought the prelude to a homosexual pick-up. Supporters of the visiting team sit among the home fans, and will receive little worse than some jovial banter. On the odd occasion that minor ructions break out at baseball stadia, this tends to be reported in fearful, hushed tones: 'There are fears that European-style sports violence may be coming to the United States following a fight in Kansas City when two men were hurt by an empty beer can.' This in spite of the fact that some older stadia are in the more dangerous parts of the big cities, where serious, professional mayhem occurs every night.

Unlike the baseball writers, the fans at the game seem less interested in topics such as the cosmic *anomie* than in the food. Baseball fans do love browsing and sluicing. After a couple of innings or so (each side plays nine) the stands begin to empty. This is in spite of the fact that throughout the game vendors patrol the walkways, calling 'Get your hot dogs, they're red hot!', or 'Never fear, I got ice-cold beer!' These limited choices are not enough. To get the full culinary range, you have to go behind the seats to the 'concession' stands, a vast covered market of comestibles, a souk of fast food.

There are hot dogs and burgers, and sandwiches and pizza and chilli, and 'crackerjack' candy and popcorn and every kind of soda. There are nacho chips, which are corn crisps covered with molten cheese sauce and topped with jalapeño peppers so fiery that your eyes water for hours afterwards. There are regional specialities: bratwurst in the Midwest, crab cakes in Baltimore, tofu and health food in California.

By the fourth or fifth inning, halfway through the game, the queues at the stands snake round the stadium's gangways. At most places you need to stand in a separate line for each different item, so you could spend the best part of the game merely refuelling yourself and your party. Luckily each concession has its own closed circuit TV, so you don't actually miss the game. Indeed you have all the comforts of home without ever leaving the stadium.

The result is that when you return to your seat, you can look along the row of your fellow fans and see a collection of bellies which would incite lust in the most torpid Turkish sultan. Bare bellies, bellies in T-shirts, bellies in cling-tight polyester, bellies with yet more food balanced upon them. Now and again a belly will quiver as its owner, spying a vendor, cries 'Hey, beer!' or 'Yo! Hot dog!' If you walk down the crowded row of a theatre, people move their feet and legs. Here they take a deep breath.

I think what I find most attractive about baseball is its very sameness, the soothing rituals which never vary, and against which the details of an individual game stand out the more strongly. Before each ball is pitched, the scene is frozen, the pitcher moves into his wind-up, throws, and it's as if he'd put his penny in the end of the pier machine. Everyone leaps into action. If the batter hits the ball, fielders rush into their predestined slots, the ball is picked up, and thrown with the force and accuracy of a rifle shot towards the appropriate base. Five seconds later, the figurines are immobile again, as if the last few moments had been a short, bewildering dream.

I love the rituals, the essential rites of each game. I like the way the organ always plays 'Take Me Out to the Ball Game', the way the umpire constantly dusts home plate with the little broom he carries for the purpose, like a neurotic housekeeper. I like the 'Seventh Inning Stretch' when the fans do unnerving, belly-wobbling exercises before their team bats for the seventh time. When the ball is hit into the stands, whoever catches it can keep it, so small boys bring their mitts from home. They have maybe a one in five thousand chance of catching a stray ball, but if they did, it would have magical powers, having been once hit by a major league player. When a spectator makes a good catch, the public announcer will almost always say, 'Give that fan a contract!'

These small rituals must have a soothing effect. Certainly a baseball crowd always seems cheerful, even when the home team has lost. The mild aggression seems stylized, directed more at the umpires than at the rival teams. Or maybe they are all full of too much food to care. I watched lowly Cleveland lose to the hated Yankees, and at the end the crowd streamed happily out, possibly reflecting on baseball as a reflection of existential ontology, or just looking for the nearest pizza parlour for another snack.

Other sports are less placid. Hockey, for example (which is what we call ice hockey), attracts fans almost entirely with the promise of violence between the players. The game is so fast that it's almost impossible to follow the puck (which cannot be seen at all on television) so the fisticuffs are pretty well all there is to watch. There might be a case for abolishing the puck altogether, except that it does make it possible for the game to end with a 'score', not that anyone seems to care very much what that is.

The top players tend to be French Canadians, and some have the violent, brooding air of men who have spent the last few weeks in some Quebec forest camp and have arrived in town to get drunk. The sports news periodically contains some item like this: 'Top hockey pro Gilles Bourassa, who took a chain saw to an opponent, cut off both his legs and gouged out his eyes, has been

157

suspended for five games. The suspension is a blow to the Peoria Widowmakers, who had hoped to assassinate all their opponents by the end of the season. A League spokesman explained that the severity of the penalty was because it was Bourassa's second offence in a week.'

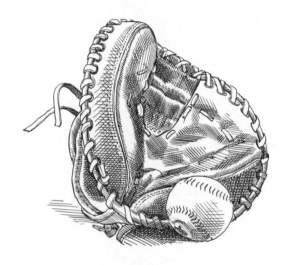

NINE

Busman's Vacation

The art of the vacation is well advanced in the United States. No doubt there are Americans who like to lie on a beach for two weeks. This is the European idea of a holiday, and it has its adherents in the US. But for most people there, a vacation means effort. There are duties to perform, things which must be seen, activities which have to be undertaken. Watch an American tourist in a European city. He or she will be studying a guidebook, working out where the next site is to be found. It's the Europeans who are sitting in the pavement cafés, sipping a *menthe à l'eau* or an espresso while the world goes past them. Americans go past the world.

They are, contrary to their own opinion, among the most hard-working people on earth. This means that they get very short vacations, so when they do have them, they like to use time to the fullest. One of the sternest duties incumbent on a parent is to go to Disneyland, or Disney World in Florida, which has more visitors each year than Canada has inhabitants.

Disney World has acquired by now something of the air of a national shrine. American parents who don't take their children there sense obscurely that they have failed in some fundamental way, like Muslims who never made it to Mecca. The Disney characters are national symbols even though they have a corporeal existence only as gigantic fibre-glass heads, usually on top of students who are working their way through college. When did you last see Mickey Mouse in a film? Have you ever seen Mickey Mouse in any film? Or Pluto? Or Goofy? The characters have become the nation's *lares* and *penates*, its household gods. When President Bush began his election campaign proper in 1988 he stood on a platform flanked by people in fibre-glass heads pretending to be Disney creations. (Some time later, to his considerable annoyance, he was flanked by people in fibre-glass raisin suits, pretending to be Californian raisins. What Bush, who was raised on the east coast, doesn't realize, is that the Californian Raisins have speedily acquired some of the same symbolic, mythic role in California as Disney characters have in the nation as a whole.)

Even other countries' favourite characters are press-ganged into serving Disney. There's a line in one of Disney's Winnie-the-Pooh films in which some character says: 'That Tigger, why, he's one taco short of a combination platter!' – a line rarely uttered in the Home Counties England of A. A. Milne. For years it was an article of conviction among the kind of people who believe what they are told in bars that Disney himself was still alive, having been quick frozen, to wait in suspended animation until they found a cure for whatever illness he died from. So in the folk consciousness he's still there, perfectly preserved, like Lenin in Red Square or Chairman Mao in Beijing. Only waiting to rise again.

In all those articles about how much Russians like queueing, even when they don't know what's at the end of the queue, I've detected a note of envy: for the camaraderie, the brief feeling of community, the agreeable sense of edging, minute by minute, nearer to your goal. The fact is that Americans adore queueing. Normally they believe – and usually they're quite right – that they are much too busy to queue. On vacation, however, they can go to Disney World and queue to their heart's fulfilment. It is a vast theme park devoted to the joys of waiting in line.

This is what happened to us on our first morning. We drove the eight miles from our hotel to the gates of Disney World. After seven miles we joined up with a queue of cars waiting for the parking lot toll booths. Once inside, we queued with all the other cars to be slotted into our appointed places. (Disney World depends on everyone doing exactly what he or she is told. One fellow near us insouciantly parked his car somewhere more convenient for him and his family. The attendant couldn't cope. His arms and legs began to wave, independent of each other. Terminal astonishment at someone demonstrating free will had caused him to lose his own motor control.)

Then you line up for a tram affair which takes you to the entry booths, where of course you queue to buy tickets. These are not cheap, but to *aficionados* of queueing they are worth every cent. Once inside, you queue to join the monorail, which whisks you straight to the heart of the park, a veritable snakepit of queues, many sinuously curved around each other. The British like to think they are good at standing patiently in line. How wrong they are! Queueing is still in its Third World infancy in Britain. We decided to relax, stand up, and see how the masters of the craft perform.

We headed for Adventureland, where we found several tempting lines. You couldn't always tell which was which, and on the Russian housewife principle, even people in the queues didn't always know, since they had simply joined in the hope that there was something exciting at the other end. At one point we thought we were waiting for the famous Jungle Cruise. But word came down the line that this was actually for the Swiss Family Robinson Tree House. So we went instead to the Pirates of the Caribbean ride, where a notice at the head of the queue promised a fifty-minute wait. Not ideal, and not the longest in the park, but a promising start.

What was gratifying about this queue was that after half an hour you reached a kind of gateway where, you assume, the queue must end. But it doesn't. There's at least half an hour more filing fun to come. The ride itself, in a boat which carries you past animatronic pirates and mock naval battles, lasts only nine minutes, so you haven't wasted too much precious time between queues.

Next we took our little girl to Fantasyland, and the queue for the carousel. A disappointing fifteen-minute wait there. Lunch was getting close, so we didn't have time to join the one-hour line for Dumbo the Flying Elephant, though that ride is only two or three minutes long, offering a splendid queue-to-ride ratio.

Our morning session in the Magic Kingdom lasted two and a half hours. Here's how it broke down:

161

Time spent queueing: 110 minutes
Time spent walking between rides: 28 minutes
Time actually spent on rides: 12 minutes

The joy of the Disney system is that there are queues everywhere, including at the lesser attractions. For some reason, only the keenest enthusiasts are willing to wait for more than an hour or so – even for the most popular attractions, such as the Space Mountain and the Haunted Mansion. This means that the queues spread out to the rides no one has really heard of, and which could be found in any travelling carnival anywhere in the country. The queues do shorten, disappointingly, as the evening draws on. We got on to the It's A Small World ride without any queueing at all, but Disney World invariably has another trick up its sleeve. At the end we had to queue to get off.

Because Disney World is one of the holy places of America, the food has to reflect this. Those who want fancy foreign food can go to the Epcot Center nearby, where in the various national pavilions, you can obtain decent French and Italian meals, or, in the English pub, Scotch eggs which, had they been available to the British artillery at Sevastopol, would have produced a different result on the day for the Light Brigade.

In Disney World you eat American. At the Refreshment Corner in Main Street USA you can get a selection of hot dogs and Coke. Or try the Town Square Café, where there is always plenty of Coke to wash down the hamburgers. In Adventureland, the colourful El Piratos y el Perico offers hot dogs and Coke. Or join the line for the exotic South Seas ambience of the Veranda Café, which serves a tempting selection of hamburgers, hot dogs and Coke. Over in Frontierland, few could resist waiting amid the rootin', tootin' excitement of Pecos Bill's Café, where the barkeep'll be happy to serve you hamburgers, hot dogs and Coke, all in an authentic Wild West saloon atmosphere.

Disney World is not merely a theme park; it represents the quintessence of America to itself. It's not a great exaggeration to say that it plays something of the same role in the American consciousness as Mecca does to a devout Muslim. The visit is planned for months or years in advance, large sums of money are put aside to pay for it, and there is a real sense of pilgrimage. The fibre-glass Mickey, Goofy and Pluto are the priests, casting their benison upon the visiting families, patting children on the head in the manner of a blessing. No alcohol is permitted, so the atmosphere is curiously hushed. At a regular carnival there is noise and bustle and whooping; at Disney World there is this eerie calm as people stand patiently in the interminable lines, like the faithful waiting for the moment of benediction. Americans commonly say that going to one of the Disney parks is something you have to do 'once in your life', and when they return there's often a sense of relief, as if to say, 'Well, that's out of the way, we don't have to do that again.'

The Disney parks are the most celebrated: the St Peter's of the theme park world. But there are many others, which may lack the same near-religious status but are enormously popular nevertheless. On the whole they are also more exciting. Currently they are engaged in a struggle to find the most thrilling ride of them all. Take Free Fall at the Magic Mountain amusement park near Los Angeles. This gives you a similar experience to, as I imagine, being hanged.

At the end of the queue you are quickly ushered into a long thin cage with space for four people (Pierrepoint, the public executioner, claimed that his victim would be dead just twenty seconds after he had shaken his hand. The staff at Magic Mountain could make the same proud boast.) You stand up, facing the front, and behind you there is thick padding the length of your body.

When your turn arrives, you're cranked back along a short track, then whisked with alarming speed up a ten-storey steel tower. At the very top you pause, then with a horrible suddenness, the cage jerks forward and is poised above the abyss. There's a wait, which seemed like half an hour, but was probably only a few nano-seconds (the scientific definition of a 'nano-second' being that period of time between a traffic light changing to green and a New York cab driver behind you blowing his horn).

This period of time was, however, long enough for the young

man next to me to speak for us all when he screamed, in apparently genuine terror, 'Assholes!'

I am not clear what happened next, since I had my eyes shut and my brain was entirely occupied by the fear that very shortly my stomach was going to pass through it. A scrutiny of earlier riders, however, suggested that we had plummeted 100 feet or so, and then slid to a halt, flat on our backs.

People clearly enjoy this. Why? They also enjoy the equal terrors of the roller coaster. The United States is currently in the grip of what is sometimes termed 'roller coaster mania'. The result is that around a hundred new ones are being built every year. Each summer, one new coaster is declared the most advanced and thrilling ever built. When I investigated the topic, the state-of-the-art coaster was said to be The Magnum, which is at Cedar Point, Ohio, and is claimed to be the tallest (201 feet) and the fastest (70 m.p.h.) ever built.

Like a guillotine, The Magnum is both sinister and elegant. The track is supported by a simple and minimal trellis arrangement, so that the two main drops (it's the first drop which is the world's highest and steepest) have a tremendous, sinuous grace.

This aesthetic judgement is not the one you necessarily feel when first sitting on the thing. There's an agonizing climb to the first peak, as the train rises 200 feet along just 400 feet of track. At the top, you look down on what appears, thanks to a trick of the eye, to be a sheer vertical fall. At this point my mind blanked out except for one terrifying question: 'How do I keep the car keys safe?'

The first serious roller coaster I ever rode was at Knott's Berry park, the quaintly named funfair in Los Angeles. On the Montezooma's Revenge ride I sat next to a young woman to whom, by way of conversation, I said, 'Do you feel as scared as I do?' She tucked her gum into the side of her cheek, then said: 'No, I rode it eight times already. I guess I like the way you figure your head is gonna come out through your ass.'

These parks, like Disney World and Disney Land, are probably the world's greatest roadside attractions. But they are only the apex of an enormous pyramid of fun. In Europe, where distances are short and most journeys can be managed in a day, there are few of these sirens designed to lure you from the highway. In America there are thousands. What's encouraging is the way that they have survived. The super-highways discourage anyone from leaving, though until 1965 it was permitted to advertise alongside them, so that parents could be nagged by their offspring for as much as 200 miles before they actually reached the exit for the Weeki Watchee Underwater Showgirls of Florida or the Barbi Doll Hall of Fame in Palo Alto, California. Now you need to know beforehand that the World's Largest Ball of Twine is in Darwin, Minnesota (leave I-94 at the St Cloud exit, then 40 miles south) or that LaCrosse, Kansas, is home to the Barbed Wire Museum (I-70 to Hays, then US 183). Occasionally someone manages to get a poster up; we once passed an imploring sign in the Midwest: 'Exit here, for world's largest collection of farming implement seats'.

Yet the huge increase in the number of travellers has kept many of these attractions going even if a few have crumbled and died. The Cursed Pyramid of Bedford, Indiana. The Shuffleboard Hall of Fame. The Diving Pigs of Aquarena, Texas. At John Wayne's Birthplace in Winterset, Iowa, you can see the eyepatch he wore while filming *True Grit*. In Meade, Kansas, you can see the Dalton Gang's hideout; in Salem, Massachusetts, the Witches' Dungeon. The Cypress Knee Museum in Palmdale, Florida, has the world's largest collection of curiously shaped pieces of cypress wood. Or so they claim. Being the biggest is crucial for these attractions. Far better to have the 'World's Biggest Dust Bunny' than 'World's Second Largest Collection of Fabergé Eggs' or 'Modest Assemblage of Van Goghs'.

Americans are as fascinated by American culture as we are. You can visit the first ever McDonald's hamburger restaurant, with the original prices intact. At the Colonel Sanders museum in Louisville, Kentucky, you can see a wire sculpture chicken which flaps its wings and lays golden eggs. There is the official Tupperware Museum in Kissimmee, Florida, where you can tour a house in which almost everything is made of Tupperware. There are Tupperware vases and Tupperware table settings and

Tupperware toys. The display fridge alone contains 119 items of Tupperware. You half-expect to see the family somewhere, stowed safely away in airtight Tupperware. Maybe they're keeping Walt Disney, in his freezer, wrapped in Tupperware; after all, Disney World is only a few miles away. At the end they show you their museum of food containers through the ages, including a 6,000-year-old Egyptian pot, Meissen ware and a Ming bowl. The climax is a complete run of modern Tupperware, to which the earlier stuff was only leading up. Greek amphora didn't stack, Sèvres porcelain couldn't be burped, and none of it was dishwasher proof.

Several towns are composed of little other than roadside attractions. Take Gatlinburg, Tennessee, which is just outside the Great Smokey Mountains National Park. It includes the Elvis Hall of Fame, where you can see his rings, his bible, his limousine and his sunglasses. At the World of Illusions they have a bronzed hologram of Elvis, singing some of his great hits. Elsewhere you can pay to be pictured on the cover of famous magazines, as *Time*'s 'Man of the Year' or this month's *Penthouse* pet. Another exhibit shows Superman using his X-ray vision to peer at Lois Lane's knickers.

The Liberace Museum in Las Vegas is another shrine. It is run to perpetuate the Memory by the pianist's brother, George, and includes scores of artifacts related to his career, though nothing about his equally colourful love life. There are cars, a model of his oil well, and a gigantic 115,000-carat rhinestone. The high spot, at least for most of the people who arrive here in double-knit polyester clothing, is the display of his fabulous stage costumes, mounted on mannequins which look vaguely like him. Weirdly, these have had sequins sewn on to their faces, so it looks as if Lee was in the last stages of some terrible skin disease.

The biggest egos in America (Los Angeles notwithstanding) are to be found in Nashville, the centre of the Country music industry. It doesn't take much to be a megastar in Nashville – a couple of hits on the Country chart should suffice – and a megastar requires a personal museum. Curiously enough, one of the greatest stars there – at least at his own valuation – is Conway Twitty, whom most people remember only for his big hit 'It's Only Make Believe', which he starts off in a leonine growl and ends up at the top of the register as if someone had just grabbed his testicles.

It turns out that Conway has had limitless hits on the Country chart, and every day of the year hundreds of his fans arrive at his home in Tennessee, aptly known as 'Twitty City'. This is a mausoleum to someone still living, a temple to the Id as big as the Ritz. For your 8 dollar entrance fee, you get to see dioramas depicting Conway's boyhood, his car, his gold records, his tour buses, and illuminated cut-outs of members of his band introduced by a six-foot-high, talking 'Twitty Bird', Conway's personal symbol.

Afterwards, you are allowed to view his twenty-four-room mansion, from a respectful distance, of course, plus the homes he built for his children and for his mother. There was much excitement among the tour party I joined when the guide said he thought he had spotted the back of Conway's head, bobbing around in the business office. Sadly, it turned out to be the back of Conway's accountant's head. But all was not lost; we could finish in the gift shop, browsing through the large selection of Conway Twitty records, tapes, hats, mugs, plaques and adoring biographies.

Americans will fly great distances to gamble. I have always thought of Las Vegas as a curiously innocent kind of town, though I am aware that many of the people who run the place may not themselves share this particular quality in abundance. But there is a certain naïvety to the clientele. Go to a European casino, in Monte Carlo perhaps, and there is a glossy, sophisticated, decadent splendour. In Las Vegas there are fat people in synthetic fabrics who spark as they walk across the floor.

Outside, in the State of Nevada, a kind of legalized anarchy prevails. The day I arrived two items in the local paper caught my eye: a man had been found in the Las Vegas zoo having sex with a nanny goat. He was not charged with this offence, since there is nothing in the Nevada penal code which specifically makes it illegal to have sex with a nanny goat in the zoo. The same day the State health administrator said that all prostitutes in the (legal) brothels would be tested for the HIV virus. But if the tests proved positive, the girls would not have to quit the trade. This would be left up to the brothel owners and the free market to decide, an extension of Thatcherism which might even give pause to Mrs Thatcher. The magazine *Soldier of Fortune*, ostensibly published for mercenary soldiers, actually purchased by wild-eyed fantasists, always holds its annual convention in Las Vegas, since Nevada is probably the only State where you are allowed to carry, across a hotel lobby, enough artillery to wipe out a small division.

Atlantic City is even more surprising. I went there by train and found I had to walk through one of the more frightening slums in America to get to the long thin strip where the casinos can be found. Atlantic City is, even more than New York, the world capital of Donald Trump – or was, until his recent difficulties. Residents of, say, the Trump Parc apartments in New York could catch the Trumpair helicopter to Atlantic City and disport themselves in the Trump Castle Hotel, or the Trump Plaza, or the new Trump Taj Mahal, which is naturally much bigger than its inferior prototype in India. High rollers could obtain special privileges by possessing the 'Trump Card'. Why not? The plan is that he is going to get all your money sooner or later, so you might as well have some of his lobster in the meantime. Karl Marx wrote that the state would wither away; what he didn't foresee was that it would be replaced by Donald Trump. In 1990, like Eastern European communism, Trump too appeared to crumble.

There is not much that is chic about Atlantic City. Caesar's Palace owes more to the aesthetic sense of the late Cecil B. De Mille than to Julius. The cabaret is called the Circus Maximus, and the Appian Way is an indoor shopping mall. Caesar's offers 'gourmet Chinese cuisine and after-dinner massage', possibly so they can double check whether you still have some money lodged about your person.

The casinos look almost identical, apart from the strange and unique uniforms. For instance, at the Sands the women wear tailcoats and tights so they look as if, in a fit of collective amnesia, they have all forgotten their trousers. The interiors are brilliantly lit, and the security heavies (you can spot them by their earpiece radios, and by their suits, which – perhaps by law – must contain at least 10 per cent natural fibre) actually need their dark glasses to see. Nowhere is better illuminated than the cash dispensers, which your credit card will persuade to disgorge money at a modest commission of about 20 per cent. The casinos also sell their own credit cards, which you slide into the fruit machines. In this dreamy, unreal world, who could resist pulling the handle time and time again? A month later, you come home from work and find the bill . . .

The knack in Atlantic City, Las Vegas and Reno (the gambling towns of Nevada depend on which big city they are nearest to; Las Vegas serves Los Angeles, Reno serves San Francisco, and the State of Idaho is served by a place called Jackpot, which is little more than a filling station and a couple of cafés, filled with fruit machines) is to take your money, but slowly. The 'slots' keep around 15 per cent of what is fed into them, so the players get most of their coins back, in dribs and drabs, and very occasionally in jackpots. Generally they stuff it straight back into the machine. The result is that 100 dollars in quarters will allow you to pull the handle 2,660 times before it's all gone. Old ladies feverishly shovel the cash in, and at first you think they must have lost their minds. But the maths shows that they have to work fast, in order to lose all their money before the bus goes back to New York, Washington or Philadelphia.

An important part of the piety of being an American is discovering America. This, along with paying the obligatory visit to Disney World, is a parent's bounden duty. You pile into the station wagon (or the giant recreational vehicle, of which more later) and set off on the highway. Naturally the place you want to reach, the very symbol of American scenic beauty, is the Grand Canyon.

It is a shock therefore to find that the Grand Canyon is full of Germans. Well, not the Canyon itself, though plenty of Germans have made their way down there, climbing into every unexpected crevice and cranny, like ants at a picnic. Walk along the miles of magnificent trails by the edge of the Canyon, and you will see healthy-looking persons of a certain age who merrily cry out 'Guten tag!' as you pass. Some wear leather shorts.

169

Our camp site, a mile or so from the Canyon rim, was crammed with Germans. They arrived in 'Rotels', the triple-decker buses which have seats in the front and three tiers of bedrooms in the back, each one just high enough for a medium-sized person to sit up in. Many of them, oblivious to the mere natives outside, would fail to draw the curtains at bedtime, so that in the luminescent dusk one could gaze at the scenic grandeur of northern Arizona in the distance, and in the foreground watch a German person trying to struggle into his nightwear without actually leaving the bunk or banging his head. At mealtimes, the bus driver erected a sort of open-sided marquee where they could eat huge steaks and wear jokey cowboy hats, making themselves look more authentically Western than the locals, who these days tend to eat quiche and wear designer shirts from the local Ralph Lauren factory outlet.

In the shower they would address you in their own language. When you failed to understand, they would say it again, only slower and louder. This is what the British used to do when they were top nation, and the Americans did later, when they took over that position. Now the Germans are doing it to the Anglo-Saxon countries, in that faintly patronizing way which one associates with district commissioners. 'We've learned some of your funny language,' it seems to say, 'now you have to learn ours.' Soon, no doubt, there will be humiliating signs in German everywhere: '*Turisten! Hier ist bier und bratwurst!*', written acknowledgment of economic superiority.

It's easy to mock the vast 'Rotels' (and fun, too) but in a sense they are only the modern version of a wagon train, without the threat of Indian attacks. And we were in no position to laugh, because we were driving round in a vast 33-foot-long 'Winnebago' motor home, or 'recreational vehicle' as they are called. These monsters ('The Beast' we always called whichever one we had) are devoted to the notion that it should be possible for an American to live in a truck and miss none of the comforts of home. Each one had a fridge and a freezer on top, an oven, hob and microwave, plus shower and a little tub which you could sit in for a bath. And a stereo tapedeck, of course, and lots of tasselled curtains and plush velour, so that the inside of each Beast looked like the cocktail lounge of a provincial hotel.

Every day we would drive to the most fabulous scenery in America, then ruin it by parking in front. At night we would retire to an RV campsite and 'hook up' The Beast to its lifelines of water, electricity and sewage. The row of similar monsters gave the appearance of a herd of elephants at dusk, drinking at the water hole. Many fellow RV'ers were retired folk who live nowhere else, moving south to Florida for the winter, then north to cooler climes in summer. Many had bumper stickers reading 'We're Spending Our Children's Inheritance'. Inside they had TVs (many camp sites offer a fourth hook-up, cable television) and videos. There would be antimacassars on the seats, and ornaments set into holes, so that they don't crash to the floor every time the van takes a turn.

At a busy time of the season, the sight of several dozen Beasts lined up in a car-park outside a National Park visitor centre is astounding. You feel a little as the early settlers must have done on seeing their first herd of buffalo. The size! The power! The numbers! On the roads, these gigantic piles of aluminium hurtle past mere motorists. Once in Texas I was driving down a long straight road, and saw in the shimmery distance a real house barrelling towards us. This was, presumably, someone who was moving home and had simply loaded their house on to the back of a flatbed truck. But a Winnebago in full sail is scarcely smaller.

Wouldn't it be simpler, one might reflect, to keep all these home comforts stationary, placed at convenient intervals around the country, and have people simply drive between them? These arrangements do exist. They're called hotels. But an RV answers some deeper need, some compulsion to find the ultimate freedom which, at bottom, all Americans crave; freedom so great that you can take that symbol of all that is still, solid and secure – your homestead itself – out on the road to wander where you will.

America's National Parks are among the glories of the world. No other country, even Canada, can claim such an astounding variety and range of scenery, so fabulously well preserved. One could argue that the National Parks Service, far from being negligent in its duty, is a trifle too fussy, too anxious that you should not set a foot astray. Everywhere you go, even in the wildest land, there are trails, well blazed and colour coded. They have trails for the blind, who are guided by ropes. Braille signs suggest that they stop at various points to feel the textures or to smell the vegetation. (One can imagine a Charles Adamms version, which tells them to sniff the poison ivy and put their hands into bushes frequented by snakes.)

The National Parks Service adores scary signs, as do the visitors, who enjoy the *frisson* of living near danger. 'Warning. Bear Country. Protect your property and food', it says in the Shenandoah National Park, an hour or so's drive from Washington. Near the summit of Mount Washington, the highest point in the North-east, a notice declares: 'The area ahead has the worst weather in America. Many have died from exposure. Turn back now if the weather is bad.' What delight! Who, advancing upward on a warm summer morning, could not feel a thrill of self-admiration as he passed such a sign?

Another deep-seated need is to get in touch with the land, to become a part of the country. It might be called the 'Walden' myth after the work by Thoreau which is largely unread but symbolizes a hunger many Americans experience. People get hold of a rustic property, possibly a log cabin, and kit it out with the barest minimum of so-called 'civilization' – a TV perhaps, a stereo system certainly; phone, fridge, dishwasher, oven, gas-operated barbecue – the least anyone needs to survive.

Even here there is no nonsense about lying back and relaxing. The cabin will probably be near a lake, so there's fishing to do, rowing, water-skiing and learning to sailboard. There's wood to chop for the fire, brush to hack away. When Ronald Reagan went on vacation to his ranch above Santa Barbara, the travelling White House staff would issue a back-breaking list of his labours each day, much of which involved clearing brush. This was startling, given that he hardly did a stroke while in Washington; the moment he was on holiday, he apparently became a pocket Hercules. But then so do most Americans, even those who do work hard at their jobs.

This may have something to do with the institution of summer camp. All but a small minority of Americans think it barbaric to be like the British and send children away from home in term-time. They do it in holiday time instead. There can be few Americans who grew up in the middle classes who do not have dreadful memories of these places. A handful of children do enjoy them: bullies, for example, those who are athletically gifted, or those who like the unrivalled opportunities to be cruel to small animals.

But for many American children, summer camp is a time of unrelieved misery. The picture of some small urchin on the phone, pleading to be allowed to return to his parents (who are having a wonderful time at home, rising at 9 a.m., i.e. three hours late, and watching dirty videos at night) is one of the most vivid images in American life.

The camp is also by a lake, and generally has some name like Camp Witcheewatchee, designed to imply an Indian heritage, or rather to disguise the fact that no Indian would dream of living near the place because of the mosquitoes, which may not be the largest in North America but are quite big enough to steal hubcaps. The regime in a summer camp is, to be fair, not as rigorous as the Gulag, and the diet is marginally better. But the ceaseless activity, the sense that a vacation is a time for endeavour and achievement, is imprinted on the American psyche. Every year in the big cities newspapers and charities mount fund-drives to send ghetto kids to camp. The stated intention is that these children of the streets will learn the joys of cool grass, sparkling water and silent, starry skies. The unspoken assumption is that they will learn hard work, discipline and the virtues of ruthless competition, thus enabling them to take a full place in American society.

TEN

The Square-Eyed Hydra

Americans have too much TV, in the way that England has too much rain. I don't mean that they watch too much – most nationalities sit in front of the set for roughly the same number of hours each week – but that they have too much available. Some people have forty channels. It's hard to understand how unnerving it is to flick through all of these as they blur past your eyes, and realize that there is absolutely nothing you want to watch. You can end up blaming yourself, and that way madness lies.

It's difficult to fill all that time. Andy Warhol's (too) often quoted remark that everyone will be famous for fifteen minutes is way out of date. A quarter of an hour isn't anything like enough to fill the time needed for everyone to be famous in. These days we all have to be famous for hours on end.

When we lived in the States I appeared on TV. My wife appeared on TV. Nearly all our friends appeared on TV, though one or two might have missed out, being away at the beach when the call came. I had a friend, a quiet scholarly fellow who preferred to spend his days with his books and his old typewriter. I never thought I would ever see him on TV. I was wrong. There he was, during the local public broadcasting station bi-annual fund-raising drive, handing out free copies of his book in exchange for pledges. This went on for hours.

Like all foreign reporters, I was expected to appear on cable television. This was a sort of duty to one's hosts, a little like being a visiting choir from a distant land; you're supposed to give an interview saying how marvellous it is to be there, and bringing messages of peace from all your peoples.

Take C-Span, the cable network which offers live coverage of the Senate and the House of Representatives. Regrettably these bodies do not sit for twenty-four hours a day, all year round, so C-Span fills the void by bringing in hacks like me who will spout happily about almost anything, for hours on end.

They have phone-ins. People are actually awake at 4.45 a.m. in California and want to call you at 7.45 in Washington to tell you exactly what they think about a bunch of foreign jerks running down their country (which means you have just taken issue with the administration over some minor point of foreign policy) and if you don't like it then you can go back home to socialist Britain.

Another caller accused me, and my colleagues, of being 'trapped in a post-Hegelian time warp', a remark which could start a brawl in any bar in the world, or at least in Oxford or Tubingen. One's reaction is of rage. Do they imagine that you actually want to be in this hot, foetid studio, providing them with an adrenalin high which they could get more easily from listed substances? Do they realize that the only form of payment for appearing is to be given a free mug, which may well be the origin of the term?

Now and again people who go on C-Span programmes make pathetic attempts to leave. 'May I go know?' they ask. 'Just a le-e-etle while longer,' say the calm, assured young women who look after you. An hour later you are still there. You stutter something about losing your job if you don't reappear in the office some time that day. 'Not long now,' they say cheerily. You begin to feel like the Evelyn Waugh character trapped in the jungle by the Dickens-loving maniac. What have they told the search parties? 'We're so sorry, but he died on air. He would have wanted it that way. Here's his mug.'

Amazingly, lots of people watch this stuff. I've received polite critiques of my performance from tourists in West Virginia, a redneck with a cap advertising his own cesspit cleaning service, and a professor in Boulder, Colorado. But then appearing on C-Span is a bit like standing around Oxford Street with a sandwich board; sooner or later everyone is going to notice you. They can't really avoid you, even if they only glimpse you while channel-hopping in search of anything worth watching on the other thirty-nine stations.

The networks are more succinct. The first time I went on *NBC News*, a full team consisting of a reporter, cameraman, lighting and sound man appeared in our apartment. They spent half an hour setting up the equipment. They then interviewed me at great length on British policy towards something or other. The questioning was so searching that, afterwards, I felt I could have passed straight into the highest grade of the Foreign Service. Then they left.

That night friends phoned to say that they thought they had seen me on the NBC news show, but that since the appearance had been so brief, they had not had time to read the caption on the screen giving my name. Could I confirm it? I later learned that I had been allowed to say: 'Mrs Thatcher won't like it.'

The most demanding of all is CNN, the Cable News Network. I should stress that I was not invited to appear on this because of any great broadcasting skill, and certainly not as a tribute to my deep knowledge of the subject in hand, but because in previous appearances I had not made any racist remarks, picked my nose, or used the opportunity to hypnotize viewers into making their wills over to me. With so much time to fill, these qualifications are enough.

American news television operates on the principle that the anchorman must never be permitted to look stupid, even if he is. Especially if he is. Like an attorney in court, he needs to know precisely what answers he can expect to each question. The questions are framed only after the answers have already been discovered. If you appear on CNN you first get a phone call from the network's headquarters in Atlanta. In the course of half an hour you are asked everything which might conceivably be relevant to the subject. Only the questions which make you come up with the best answers are selected. This makes for a smooth interview. If you changed your mind about something, the process would grind to a halt. CNN would have to go off the air. Viewers might think that the studio had been hijacked by terrorists.

None of these stations pays anything as vulgar as money. It would be thought demeaning. They will, however, send a limousine, even if your office is just across the street. It's assumed that the sight of a Cadillac slightly longer than a city bus arriving to pick you up will increase your prestige at your place of work far more than any mere cash which they might pay you. Who needs it? Even people who *aren't* celebrities often have money. Once inside the mobile lounge you have perhaps thirty seconds to enjoy the colour TV, the stereo radio and tape deck, the cocktail cabinet, semi-circular velour sofas, the bowl of roses and the small library of current magazines. Unless your office is more than ten blocks away, in which case it might be worth opening that bottle of chilled champagne.

There may be no money, but you do get a lovely letter. Once I went on the *CBS Morning News*, a show which had created much the same enthusiasm among the ratings as Captain Bligh once did. I was being interviewed about the British Royal Family by Maria Shriver, who is now Mrs Arnold Schwarzenegger. A few days later I received a letter, personally word-processed by her, saying (and I quote from memory), 'Thank you so much for your stimulating contribution to our discussion about the British Royal Family. We hope very much that you will be able to join us again the next time this topic is on our agenda.'

One can imagine the result if she had written a similar letter to her plumber, thanking him for his stimulating contribution to the burst pipe problem but not offering to pay the bill. He'd have her in court before you can say 'Schwarzenegger', which most people can't.

On some American shows, the guests are expected to attack each other, ltke pit bulls. This can be confusing for a Briton, since our style is to deflect antagonism. If someone argues Stalin was right to exterminate the kulaks, you're supposed to mutter something like, 'Not entirely sure that I share that view . . . slight difference of opinion here, I suspect . . .'

Not so on *Crossfire*, CNN's daily warathon, which is watched in – they say – about half a million homes a night. There are two resident hosts, one left-wing, the other right, and two guests similarly paired. I was supposed to be the soggy liberal guest. The topic was whether Vladimir Pozner, a Soviet apologist, should be allowed to appear on American TV (how distant, how nostalgic,

those days seem to be!). My suspicion was that the carpet-biters on the American Right feared Pozner because he had been raised in Los Angeles and had a flawless American accent, which made him sound much more convincing than the usual heavy-jowled Russian, who in those days usually looked as if his suit had been run up from cement.

On my left was a cuckoo Republican congressman called Bob Dornan, and on the other side the programme's in-house liberal, one Tom Braden, whose wife later wrote a book describing her seemingly innumerable affairs in and around Washington. So I was stuck between the city's loopiest legislator and its most celebrated cuckold. On a monitor, his beady visage beamed in from New York, was the then editor of the far right magazine the *National Review*, William Rusher, a man who struck me, in the Irish phrase, as being 'wired to the moon'.

Everyone chatted quite amicably until the lights went up, when suddenly Braden made a ferocious attack on Dornan, who, it appeared, had called Pozner 'a little Jew' in the House that day. Dornan tried to claim that this remark was not anti-Semitic; he had merely meant that Pozner was (a) of diminished stature, and (b) a traitor to his race. Braden snorted like a stallion. 'Why doncha take a look inside your soul, Bob,' he said, 'because I don't think you're gonna like what you see.'

Things got steadily worse. Now and again I would open my mouth, but usually not fast enough to say anything. Finally I muttered that the American people were probably clever enough to see through such obvious propaganda, at which point Rusher began to speak in what some Americans like to believe is an English accent.

'Eow, eour British friend thinks we are smart, does he, eoh may word, fraitfully grateful, aim sure!' Once or twice I tried again, but was drowned by hoots of derision, some possibly from the cameramen. Finally, thank heavens, it was over. The lights went down, Bob Dornan swung round, gazed straight into my eyes, pumped my arm, and said – bewilderingly – 'Thank you for Winston Churchill!'

As I left the studio, I heard someone ask, 'Who was that?' and

180

someone else replied, 'Oh, he's nobody, they couldn't get Sam Donaldson.' They did ask me back, a couple of years later. I pretended I was busy.

The *raison d'être* of American TV is the ads. This is a truism which happens to be true. There are people who care about making fine programmes – more than you might think – but they operate in spite of the ads. The commercials are so important that they have shows which are entirely tributes to them, a sort of Oscar ceremony for ads, during which viewers can once again enjoy their favourites, some of which they may have seen already only 1,873 times.

American adverts are more closely targeted than in most other countries, so you get a good idea of who your fellow viewers are. For instance, the morning game shows are interrupted by Lee press-on nails, Mr Ray's Hair-Weave Salon (whose customers look as if they've just stuck their finger in a socket) and job training ads. 'Hey, look at me! I earn big bucks sexing quail. Write The School of Quail Sexing . . .'

In the small hours, during the chic, smart-alec talk shows, such as *Late Night With David Letterman*, we join the glamorous world of the urban professional. Here we are roaring up the California coast in our Pontiac Sunbird. This is us in New York at 3 a.m., sharing a crisp dry Michelob beer with Eric Clapton, or hanging out with guys who wear Levi's 'Dockers', pants for the *Big Chill* generation.

The oddest phenomenon is the national news. Apparently the people who watch these shows are, on average, quite a lot older than most other viewers, so the ads are largely aimed at them, and specifically at their numerous ailments.

The local news which precedes the network news brings no hint. The ads are the usual ones: minor hometown celebrities urging you not to do crack if you're pregnant, and car dealers whose link with sanity is, at best, tenuous. 'Carl Kubitz of Kubitz Kars here! I'm slashing prices on thousands of '89 Fords! If I can't match the opposition price, I'll shoot myself! And leave you my house and land! Ha, ha!'

After the news we enter the gentle sitcom uplands, with

181

cheery families scoffing spaghetti sauce and Orville Redenbacher's gourmet-flavoured microwave popcorn, which actually exists, though you would need to be a rather strange person to go into a shop and ask for it.

But for the half-hour in between we are stranded in a world of subfusc gloom. Massacres in China, blazing rain forests and AIDS victims alternate with the more immediate horrors facing the viewers: piles, constipation, arthritis, incontinence and loose false teeth.

The effect can be of unrelenting misery. On *ABC News* Peter Jennings (the networks are trying to get young people back, so ABC chose Jennings who looks as if he probably has most of his working parts in order) will say: '. . . and the latest estimates are that up to two thousand people may have been killed. Back after this.' Fade to a doom-laden voice: 'When you've got haemorrhoids, walking is hard. Sitting, worse . . . for your haemorrhoidal itch, get "Anusol".' (This also exists, but I would expect you'd want to pronounce it to the pharmacist with great care.)

Over on CBS Dan Rather will be saying: '. . . and the search for survivors has now been called off.' Cut to unhappy fellow groaning: 'The doctor says it's heartburn.' Wife: 'Yes, and high blood pressure. You need less salt – and Rioplan Plus-2.'

The ads trade on panic among older women that their husbands will reject them and go off with a bimbo, as, in real life, many do. A middle-aged couple are having their anniversary dinner. They're smiling at each other, exposing acres of denture. A gungy voice-over says: 'It's nice to know he still likes the way you look. If you use Efferdent, *all* he'll notice is you.'

What on earth do they expect him to say? 'Good God, Luanne, after forty years of marriage you look like a beaver with a nicotine problem. No wonder I'm booked on a flight to Acapulco with my secretary first thing tomorrow'?

They've never quite figured out how explicit these ads should be. Sometimes they are disgustingly frank; sometimes it's hard to know which affliction is being addressed. My favourite of the open, or *glasnost*, school of medicinal promotion, was an old ad for Milk of Magnesia. A blue-collar worker moaned at the camera:

182

'Uh, oh, I'm all blocked up.' Then a line of girls dressed as Milk of Magnesia bottles danced on to the screen, singing a little jingle. Back to the man, who's sighing with pleasure. 'Now that's what I call relief!'

The opposite is the current approach, in which people – housewives, an airline pilot – smile into the camera and say, '*Good Morning!*' as if they had just won the lottery, or heard Nixon was dead. You couldn't know why it was such a spiffy morning until you heard the name of the product: 'Exlax'.

Incontinence pad commercials usually go for this upbeat approach. Tom Brokaw on NBC will be saying: '. . . and doctors warn there is no cure yet for the deadly disease. In our next segment, the drug menace reaches America's kindergartens. Now this', and there's a school-crossing guard laughing her head off. Why? Because she's no longer troubled by incontinence. Or married couple are out on the dance floor. He confides to her: 'It's great to be able to hold you in my arms again.' We know exactly why he couldn't until recently, but naturally they don't like to spell it out.

The makers of all these commercials have to decide whether to demonstrate the rapture shared by those who use the product, or the misery suffered by those who don't. The laughing guard and the dancing couple are better here than the alternative; say, an executive arriving at a crucial board meeting only to find the MD staring at the wet patch on his pants.

My all-time golden memory came in the 1989 presidential inauguration, at the solemn moment when Reagan was in the Capitol Building, preparing to hand his office over to George Bush. It's the equivalent, perhaps, of the signing of the register at a Royal wedding. *ABC News* took the moment to break off for an ad, which began: 'Great news, honey! I don't need surgery for my haemorrhoids!'

Since (q.v.) America is a manic-depressive nation, the ads take on a patriotic tinge when the country is feeling up about itself. Few countries in the world are then so remorselessly sold back to themselves. I'm not only referring here to the 'Made in the USA' ads in which a few has-been film stars proudly show off the 'Made

183

in the USA' label on their jackets. Everyone wants to feel patriotic, but they'd just as soon avoid paying an extra 40 dollars for the pleasure. There's another aspect too: while American nationalism loudly asserts that American is best, there's still a residual, cringing fear, possibly a growing fear, that imports – whether European or Japanese – may actually be better. This nervous ambiguity is caught in a radio ad for a brand of 'lite' beer which is made at various mass-production breweries around the US. The jingle goes: 'Twenty-five calories, never tasted so imported.' How can anything *taste* imported? What they mean is 'tastes good'.

The patriotic pitch is not usually designed to suggest that a product is actually better because it's made in the USA, merely that its purchase will associate and identify you with what's important about America. Miller beer had a Country and Western band singing to a series of stirring scenes, principally of male bonding, all hearty backslaps and handshakes, and folks with shining eyes. The song spoke of people who were 'proud and free' and 'looked you right in the eye'; a land of sincerity and honesty, where people 'care about their families'. And, naturally, 'Miller's the beer.' Nobody suggests here that Miller tastes better (this particular line is pitched in another commercial, though like most American beer, to the European palate, it tastes of nothing much at all). Nor do they imply that it will get you drunk quicker; merely that it will slap 'America' on you, like a coat of paint.

Sometimes this becomes ludicrous. Since most beer drinkers watching TV are slumped inactive on a couch or in a Lazee-Boy recliner, waiting for someone to invent a remote control for fridges, the ads have to imply that they are active, manly, hard-working and patriotic as well. One ad has a succession of military images – soldiers, monuments and so forth, with a voiceover: 'You serve your country when your country calls. Budweiser returns your salute.' Another series showed lumberjacks chopping down forests, muscle-rippling country people helping to erect a neighbour's house, while the virile choir sings: 'You make America work, and this Bud's for you.'

Chrysler Cars ran a successful campaign based on the theme:

184

'The pride is back/Born in America', which they used because Bruce Springsteen wouldn't let them have 'Born in the USA' owing to the fact that it is – if you listen to the words – a sarcastic, even bitter lament about a Vietnam veteran who returns home without a job. Also because they couldn't carol '*Made* in the USA', since many Chrysler cars are actually built in Canada. (Not that many people would notice the difference. Most maps of the US don't even acknowledge the existence of Canada, and when it is shown, it's usually on a weather chart, where it's being blamed for the arrival of freezing northerly winds. If you told some Americans that people such as Michael J. Fox, Peter Jennings and Dan Aykroyd were actually Canadians, and thus foreigners, they would suspect you were barking mad.)

General Motors hit back by calling their Chevrolet range 'The heartbeat of America', a jingle which they illustrated with heartbeat sounds, 'bump *bump* . . . bump *bump*'.

Now a Chevvy is obviously more American than, say, a Volkswagen, but why is it more American than, say, a Ford? The answer is that there is no reason at all, any more than the Atlanta Braves have the right to call themselves 'America's baseball team'. The line evokes good feelings, and that is all there is to it. (Though when the wretched Braves found themselves at the bottom of the National League, the tag was briefly changed to 'The never-say-die Atlanta Braves, America's baseball team'.) GMAC, which finances people to buy General Motors' cars, calls itself 'the official sponsor of America's dreams', implying that all Americans dream about is a new car.

Amtrak, the national rail network, doesn't suggest that its trains are comfortable, cheap or convenient, but that it will bring you closer to America than a plane ever could: 'All aboard, America, all aboard Amtrak'. United Airlines responds by asking you to 'fly the friendly skies of our land', though why they are particularly friendly for United passengers, since nowhere in the US are you likely to be brought down by a ground-to-air missile, it does not make clear.

There's a certain visionary look associated with the depiction of the American dream on TV. It is a sort of half smile, combined with an optimistic gaze, uplifted to an elevation of around 45 degrees. I have never seen it in real life, but it figures a lot on TV, quite often when someone is contemplating the purchase of a new car. Generally it's associated with the notion of future prosperity, which is an essentially American concept. Take an ad for Aetna, a financial and insurance company. We meet a young Oriental fellow, presumably a recent immigrant since his English is not too good. He is starting out with his own workshop and his white neighbour, an amiable soul but lacking the visionary, uptilted smile, is a bit of a wet blanket.

'That's the trouble with you, Bud,' says our hero. 'You're afraid to dream.'

Gazing permanently aloft, the Oriental newcomer (with the help of some astonishingly friendly Aetna advisers, who look as if they had just drifted in from a somewhat formal frat party) soon turns his atelier into a humming factory employing hundreds. Bud is converted. 'The people, the spirit, they're all the best,' he muses. But Aetna cannot bring itself to take the credit even for this success. 'One more thing, my friend,' says the entrepreneur. 'Best country.'

It's inconceivable that a British ad could employ the same pitch, at least over the past fifty years. Yet it would have been an attitude widely shared in Britain in the last century. We are more realistic now, but the loss of confidence is a real one, and perhaps a corrosive one too. If there had been TV ads in the days of Queen Victoria, you might even have seen some contented darkie starting up a small business (in his own country, of course; we didn't let them over here), and announcing proudly: 'One more thing, massa. Best Empire.'

The work ethic is also used to sell, and the heroism of labour is celebrated in the US quite as much as in any socialist realist painting. Like Budweiser, Medipren pain reliever likes to suggest that it is a reward for hard work and a means of continuing. Even a headache makes you a better American. Their ad used Carly Simon's rueful love song, 'I Haven't Got Time for the Pain', performed in a deep macho voice, over pictures of a man hammering in fence stakes, a middle-aged woman hoisting great racks of newly baked bread, and a man with muscles like ferrets fighting in a sack who is digging up the road. None of them is at all good-looking; their glamour derives entirely from their arduous jobs.

But it's not just blue-collar work which is fêted. The lone executive, hunched over his computer long after everyone else has gone home, is a familiar figure. American Airlines is fond of the image. A young man has just returned to a deserted office from what appears to have been a wearying business trip. His boss phones to say that he must leave again the next day, and suggests two AA flights, but implying that he deserves a rest and should take the later one. It turns out that the young greaser has already made a reservation on the early flight.

In another American Airlines commercial, the Stakhanovite of the computer screen is told to look in his desk drawer, where he finds his reward for all that work: a pair of AA tickets to Hawaii. (Hawaii is important here, being simultaneously utterly exotic and yet as American as Peoria, Illinois.)

Compare this to the British Airways ad, shown on both sides of the Atlantic, where head office in London plan to take advantage of an executive who's been working in their New York branch office. The overnight flight will have wrecked him – except that he wisely came British Airways Club and so is refreshed and ready to outsmart them. The Americans imply that you aim for success through hard work and loyalty to the company; the British suggest that people are more likely to try subterfuge and malice.

One of the most remarkable is a celebrated ad for United Airlines. A handsome career woman is setting off from Chicago for a day's work in New York, but first she has to say goodbye to her enchanting little daughter, who's maybe three or four. The commercial lasts only a minute, but it takes them both through their day: while the little girl is painting, her mother is making a presentation on huge sheets of paper; while the child eats peanut butter sandwiches, Mom is having a boardroom lunch. Finally, thanks to United Airlines, they are reunited at the end of the day.

Presumably they're not implying that any other airline would have seen the mother dead, especially as the ad was airing at a time when a number of United flights had come to sudden and regrettable ends. Nor was there an explicit pitch: for example, we have so many flights between important cities that you'll be able to contract your business without spending a night away from home. The idea can only have been to tie together two important strands of American life – hard work and motherhood – and to hang the airline's name on the patriotic rope.

One result of these successful advertisements is that programmes have begun to copy them. They must, to hold the viewers' attention. Take the news. There probably never was a classical age of television news, in which Ed Murrow explained the world's most intractable problems to a grateful nation, and Eric Severeid's commentaries always struck me as wordy and mistaken, but there most certainly was an era when the news was better than it is today.

What has replaced real news is something scornfully called in the US 'News McNuggets', after the McDonald's fast-food dish in which the awkwardly shaped chicken is broken down into small chunks, each with the flavour and consistency of cardboard.

The metaphor can be extended. Real news is like a fish: it's hard to grasp, it moves around a lot and when you try to consume it, you get stuck on the bones and slithery skin. McDonald's solved that problem with the 'Filet-O-Fish', a square white thing in breadcrumbs, served with tangy sauce in a convenient hand-sized bun. The new news offers 'Filet-O-Facts': all the appearance of news without any of the difficult bits, news which passes into your stomach without any of it sticking in your gullet on the way.

CBS's *60 Minutes* is the classiest version. A poignant story here, a bit of a scandal there, and the ghetto kid who went on to play at Carnegie Hall. There are elements of Esther Rantzenism in it: the team tracks down and doorsteps a defence contractor who overcharged for an Air Force coffee percolator, but it can't actually tackle the real scandal of defence procurement because that's complicated, full of figures, and might upset too many people.

But *60 Minutes* is a Harvard seminar beside the new tabloid news shows, such as *A Current Affair* and *Inside Edition*. When

188

A Current Affair sends its cameras down to Rio, it's not to investigate how the Brazilian government is tackling inflation, but to find out just how skimpy those new season's tanga swim-suits can get! Either you offer the viewers some banker in a suit, or a set of tanned wobbly bits. It's not hard to figure out which sells the most advertising. Why bother with serious sports cover-age, when you can find a nine-year-old boy in Florida who can beat the golf professionals? Who cares about rising crime when there's a poignant story about a policeman who had a hit record with his song about a slain colleague? Social problems? Forget 'em. We've got the story of a woman who risked twenty years in jail for a single night of love.

This is the TV equivalent of our own tabloid newspapers. But at least the *Sun* and the *Mirror* aren't forcing the serious papers to copy them. In the US, however, there are signs that the net-works are beginning to follow the Filet-O-Facts approach in their own news coverage. Bite-sized portions are served up with a tasty garnish of personality. What's actually happening in Beirut or Northern Ireland, or even the barrios of Los Angeles, is barely mentioned unless there's a car bomb bringing shots of bleeding children on the satellite, or a grieving Mom who lost her son in the drug wars. News around the world is a constant, bubbling, rolling stew, from which TV selects only the choicest morsels for itself. It has become like those 'grazing' restaurants in which nobody gets a full meal, only a series of brief taste sensations.

The network news is also being squeezed by cable. In Texas, I met a beautiful woman with a long, lustrous mane of yellow hair and, to judge from her conversation, more of the same between her ears. She was an 'anchor', or presenter, for the local news in some medium-sized southern city, but hoped soon to break into a 'major market' (American TV stations no longer serve viewers, but 'markets', which of course is how the advertisers see them too). She wanted advice on breaking into TV in Washington, which is the centre of the tenth largest metropolis in America. If she did, she would expect, sooner or later, to earn a million dollars a year, mainly because she was (a) beautiful, and (b) did not spray the camera with saliva every time she opened her mouth. Her knowledge of events outside her home town, indeed outside her head, struck me as more or less non-existent.

Marshall McLuhan claimed that TV was turning the world into a 'global village'. At the time he was no doubt right, but since then the opposite has occurred. Instead of TV bringing the world into our own small communities, it has imposed our village on the world. Local news, with its mini-cams and satellite uplinks, has its own people covering every important event. A party convention or a hurricane; either way a familiar local face is there interviewing the delegate from Dustpan, North Dakota, or explaining how a Caribbean hotel popular with many Dustpan people has lost a roof tile in the hurricane. Like Monty Python's 'News for Parrots' ('A plane has crashed in Switzerland. No parrots were involved') this is news for those who find it hard to let their imaginations wander away from home. 'An earthquake has obliterated the entire state of California. No word yet on how many Chicago people are involved.' 'Next. The start of World War Three and a Dallas man has been injured. Stay with us.'

The problem with American TV is, I suspect, to do with its means of funding. There is no shortage of talent there. American actors are, on the whole, much better than British. In the States actors have generally been truck drivers or waitresses or lumberjacks and have seen something of life. Ours have been to drama school.

Neither is there a shortage of money. Popular quiz shows such as *Wheel of Fortune* – the most successful of all, for this reason: the rules of the game make it sensible for a contestant to announce the answer long after he has actually worked it out, which means that the dumbest viewer has time to work out what A ST*TCH *N T*ME might be – takes millions of dollars a year, of which a minuscule proportion goes on the pitiful prizes, most of which would only be at home in a trailer park. The most famous news readers, such as Dan Rather of CBS, can earn 3 million dollars a year because they are actually worth it, in cash terms. An extra tenth of a point on the ratings is worth far more than their salaries.

The difficulty is that advertisers want bodies, and if they are slumped, comatose, upon a sofa, so much the better. The British

Spitting Image made a number of 'specials' for the US market. They got the finest reviews I have ever seen in America for a comedy show. But they were ended because the network said they were too expensive to produce.

This sounds like hooey. What probably happened was that, while the people who watched them thought they were hilarious, a significant minority found them either baffling or distasteful. Since a hundred people gazing glassily at the screen are more interesting to the advertisers than ninety laughing their heads off, they had to go. The American rip-off, *D. C. Follies*, starring the cuddly Krofft puppets, is as bland as an invalid's milk pudding. In this lame apology for satire, even Richard Nixon is a lovable old scamp. I expect you can buy him as a soft toy to put in your child's crib.

It's a cliché of British talk about television that the BBC was dragged into the modern world only by the bracing effect of commercial competition from ITV. This may be true. But it's worth pointing out that the BBC also set standards of quality, commitment and experiment, which forced ITV to run just as hard in that direction. We may have *Take Your Pick* with Michael Miles to thank for *Bob's Full House*. But we should also thank the BBC Drama Department for *Brideshead Revisited* and *The Jewel in the Crown*, which no commercial company in America could have shown, let alone made. It is only relentless fund-raising which allows them to be shown on publicly funded television, where they are enthusiastically praised by the small minority who see them.

Watch American TV and you could get the impression that the United States consists of small, cosy, nuclear families, who live surrounded by unspeakable violence. The sitcoms tend to be extremely claustrophobic. In *Family Ties*, which for years was second only to *The Cosby Show* in the ratings, the family rarely left home. The greatest tragedy the family could imagine was its older son leaving home. In *Cosby* they almost never step out of the house, except occasionally to stand on the sidewalk outside. When did the cast of *Cheers* decide to leave the bar? No one can blame them. Outside, the cop shows depict a world of unrelenting

191

mayhem. Of course Americans know that this is not the case, and that the violence, where it does exist, does not come in designer pastel colours, as on *Miami Vice*. But they are sometimes puzzled why other people around the world should imagine that this is what America is like.

The sitcoms are nearly all relentlessly upbeat. Roseanne Barr's stand-up act was harsh and bitter. 'My husband said, "Why don't we all go on a family vacation?" I said, "Sure, if you get a court order." ' But her weekly sitcom, *Roseanne*, almost always ends in a warm embrace with her husband. The show has been praised for being realistic, but in fact it is no more true to working-class life than *Cosby* reflects the world of a typical black family.

But American TV does travel. In their unending quest for a show that will prevent the largest number of people from changing channels for the longest possible time, the big production companies have made shows which cross, without visas or ideological checks, every national and language barrier. A friend of mine, a former Beirut correspondent, told me that however bad the fighting, it would always stop for the whole hour that *Dallas* was broadcast on the local TV.

(It's intriguing that American soap operas tend to be set in wealthy surroundings, whereas British series – *Coronation Street, Eastenders* – are about the lives of the poor. The Americans reflect a national aspiration for prosperity, for mobility and competition, while the British yearn for a lost sense of community and stability.)

I got an illustration of the extraordinarily wide reach of the most famous of all American soaps some many years ago, when I was working in what was still called Rhodesia. A colleague and I had just given a ride to a young white man who had recently returned from South Africa which was, to him, a dreamworld of colour TV and motorways. 'And,' he said in wonder, 'they have this amazing TV show called *Dallas*. Do you have *Dallas* in England?'

When we told him we did, he seemed disappointed, so to cheer him up we asked who he thought had shot J. R. There was a silence from the back of the car.

'Someone has shot J. R.?' he asked in horror, and we realized that he came from a culture so primitive that people were still unaware that J. R. had even been shot. In the past, anthropologists used to measure how advanced a civilization was by when it had invented the wheel, or discovered fire. Now all they need to find out is how far advanced they are in the latest American soap operas.

ELEVEN

Best Friend to the Nation

Here we are at Mount Rushmore, South Dakota, where the monstrous busts of four presidents – Washington, Jefferson, Lincoln and Theodore Roosevelt – have been carved into the rock. At one time there was a move to fit Ronald Reagan on, next to them, though some thought it would be a shame to spoil his belief that the mountain is an amazing natural phenomenon.

America loves the representations of its heroes to be not just larger than life, but stupendously, awesomely bigger than anything else. If blue whales built statues to each other they'd be smaller than these. In Washington, DC, Lincoln looks down on the puny tourists beneath him, his legs straddled, a bearded Colossus of Rhodes. On Stone Mountain, Georgia, the South's answer to Mount Rushmore, heroes of the Confederacy are carved in equal immensity. Now the fashion is for huge murals depicting Dr Martin Luther King, his face as large as the side of a house, looking earnestly down upon his children.

The United States is the first country to have invented itself, so it justifiably honours its creators. Run down the list of public holidays: Columbus, who found the place (actually, it turns out that he was a latecomer, but nobody has yet thought of a Lief Erikson Day or an allied 'Lief Erikson Day Sale featuring thousands of '89 Toyotas!'); Washington, who won the new nation's independence; Lincoln, who prevented it from being carved in two. King helped win equality, in theory at least, for all Americans, though a few States objected to his birthday being made a public holiday. So in parts of the South, it is also Stonewall Jackson Day, and inhabitants may use their free time to celebrate either the man who freed black people or one who tried to keep them in slavery.

Two of the most powerful myth figures in America are, superficially, very different men. Jefferson was a son of gentry, went to university, read the classics voraciously throughout his life, married a wealthy woman and went on to become perhaps the most brilliant of all American presidents.

Elvis Presley did none of these things. On the other hand, there are surprising similarities in the attitude their fellow countrymen hold towards them. Go to Charlottesville, Virginia, and Jefferson might still be alive. At the University of Virginia, which he founded, you are told that 'Mr Jefferson built this' or 'Mr Jefferson designed that' or 'Mr Jefferson intended that the students should be able to do the other'. It must be like being educated in Napoleon's tomb; the presence is entirely pervasive. In the town almost every other building, apart from the fast-food joints, appears to be named after Jefferson. The local paper sometimes runs lengthy correspondences in which it is debated whether Mr Jefferson would have approved the design of, say, a new shopping mall.

At Monticello, the house which he designed and had built near the town, the atmosphere is, if anything, even more hushed and reverential. The whole place is regarded as a shrine, even more than Mount Vernon, where Washington lived. All over Virginia you can visit wonderful houses built by men who wrote stirring tracts on the inalienable rights of man, while outside the slaves did the work.

At Monticello, you would scarcely be surprised if the elderly ladies who guide you round (they *never* mention his reputed black mistress) pointed out a rock by the door: 'and this is where Mr Jefferson rolled away the stone . . .'

We fell in with a family, a husband and wife who had been raised in Charlottesville but had gone to live in Seattle, in part, they said, to escape from the ever-present Jefferson worship. However, like a Jesuit education, Mr Jefferson cannot be altogether escaped in later life, and they had come back to show their daughters round.

The adoration was remorseless. The main attraction of the

195

house is the clock which Mr Jefferson designed and which was perfect in every particular, including the fact that it was possible to learn the day of the week by noting to which point on the wall the spherical weights were currently adjacent. Because there was room for only six days' movement, Mr Jefferson had cut a hole in the floorboard. The guide explained in hushed tones that when Mr Jefferson could not see the weights, he knew it must be Saturday and the clock would shortly need rewinding.

Our new friend could take it no longer. 'Yeah,' he said in a loud whisper, 'you always know it's Saturday when your balls drop through the floor.'

The same note of sustained awe is found at Graceland, Elvis's home in Memphis, Tennessee. Elvis did not design the house, which was built by a local doctor and named after his wife, but he did decide the interior décor, which is, to say the least, striking. There are tables covered in a marble-type substance to match the similarly marble-style walls, the longest white couch you have ever seen, and a 'Jungle Room' in which all the furniture is unholstered in mock animal fur and there are carved claws on the arms and legs. 'This was Elvis's personal choice,' say the guides in the reverent tones familiar from Monticello. Well, it certainly wouldn't be anyone else's choice. You are not allowed to go upstairs to the bedroom, and the one room in the house which every visitor would like to see – the bathroom where he was discovered dead – is also closed. Every house of faith must contain a sanctum sanctorum. As for Presley's drug habit, this is dismissed as an overdependence on prescription medicine and is blamed on an indulgent doctor. The keepers of the flame cannot be expected to think of Elvis as a junkie. They speak in a hushed horror of the various women who have written books or articles, claiming to have had children by him.

Out in the garden, after you have seen the famous pink Cadillac, the Stutz Bearcats and various other impractical vehicles, you are permitted to visit the graves of Elvis and his parents, guarded by a statue of Jesus, who looks down protectively upon the stones. (Presley's middle name is misspelled as 'Aaron' instead of 'Aron'; to believers, this is proof that their boy is not actually under there and the corpse is an impostor, the first Elvis lookalike to be actually dead.) The statue of Jesus, slightly smaller than the one which guards Rio, but not very much, is a clue to the Presley myth, which has several resemblances to that other great religious story. You can trace it back to the Presley birthplace, which is around a hundred miles to the south-east, in Tupelo, Mississippi. Graceland is not a large dwelling but it is lavishly appointed. The birthplace is an extremely small house which could hardly be said to be appointed at all. It has two rooms, and is a 'shotgun shack', so called because the front, back and inside doors are in line, which means that it would be possible to fire a shotgun clean through the house without hitting anything, making this the world's most curiously named architectural style, if perhaps not its most ornate.

As in many stately homes of Europe, the original furniture has long vanished, but the shack has been refitted in the style of the period, which means a few sticks of the cheapest possible furniture and a wood-burning stove. On its own it's a fascinating reminder of a past era in American life which normally no one would have bothered to think worth restoring. But this is not why people come.

The reminders of another life which began in humble sur-roundings come thick and fast: Elvis's father was also a carpenter, we learn. The family was obliged to leave home in a hurry shortly after his birth (though for different reasons; Vernon Presley couldn't keep up the payments). His mother was a much more important influence in his life than his father.

When he first began to arouse adulation in his admirers, he was reviled by the authorities. Curiously enough, many of these attacks are on display at Graceland; curious, that is, until you realize that the original hatred Presley inspired is an important element of the myth. After that he came into glory. Among his disciples was one who betrayed him – the over-generous doctor – and, of course, I could go on.

Elvis clearly had to rise again, and plenty of people believe that he did (though they don't actually go so far as to allege that he literally came back from the dead; merely that his 'death' was a ruse designed to permit him to return to a real life. Often the fantasies about what Elvis is doing with his new-found privacy have him doing ordinary, regular guy, kind of things; one sighting had him flipping burgers for a living in Michigan). There are doubters who, like Thomas, have seen him but cannot believe it. For them the 'supermarket press' prints sets of pictures which purport to *prove* that he is still amongst us. One of the most recent, apparently snapped through a telephoto lens or possibly the bottom of a Kilner jar, shows a portly man with sideburns, dark glasses and a sagging stomach, walking across a parking lot in Las Vegas. It could be Elvis, but on the other hand it could be one of at least another million portly Americans with sideburns, of a type who frequently turns up in Las Vegas.

True believers hold that Elvis 'talks' to them on cassette tapes, but these are only sent to those who are convinced he is still alive. He sings songs which were not written until after he died, though it is hard to imagine that anyone finds these especially convincing. There were plenty of Elvis imitators before and since his death, though it must be admitted that the idea does have possibilities: *Elvis Sings the Jason Donovan Songbook* would sell all round the world.

In case you doubt that the central myth of Western civilization is resonating here, consider that in some parts of the country you can buy black velvet pictures of the Madonna (no relation) holding a baby who has the face of Elvis. People get married at the birthplace, the tacky glitz of the chapel contrasting with the desperate poverty of the shack. This is America, and to be frank, one Jesus isn't enough. America invented the term 'superstar' which, when it came to mean anyone who'd had more than one hit record, had to be promoted to 'megastar'. What do you call someone for whom even that term is too trite? 'Messiah', perhaps.

Celebrity in the United States is linked to the old Greek idea of 'charisma', which meant far more than a commanding personality – it was a grace bestowed from above, and carries the unspoken notion that famous people are in some way blessed. Elvis was no more celebrated and no more popular than, say, Frank Sinatra in his day, but the mythic echoes set up by his story are more powerful and more resonant. You can be sure that when Sinatra dies there will not be thousands of people carrying lit candles past his grave every year.

Another figure whose life seems oddly illuminated is Bob Hope, who I sometimes suspect was England's revenge for the War of Independence. Hope was born in London in 1903, though his family soon emigrated to the US. He was a popular comedian, and made some amusing films. None of this accounts for the reverence in which he is held. Troops stationed abroad are obliged to attend his concerts. Scarcely a holiday occurs without a Bob Hope special on the TV. These days it is rare for a massive television event, such as the football 'Superbowl', to begin without a Tribute to Bob Hope. During the last presidential inauguration, who led the parade? Not the President, for sure. Who would have recognized him? Bob Hope, of course. There must be young Americans who believe that Hope is written into the Constitution somewhere, like the right to free speech.

All this is in spite of the fact that he has not cracked a real joke since, perhaps, 1967. An active Republican, he speaks at fund-raising dinners. Here are two of the 'jokes' he made at the expense of the Democratic candidate in 1988: 'We can't let the Greeks into the White House; they'd smash all that china!' and ' "Dukakis?" It sounds like something you step in!'

These gags are the equivalent of alcohol-free beer; they are humour-free jokes. In a sense, that is the point. Hope has long passed the stage of being a comedian, and has become instead a national emblem. For him to say anything which was actually funny (as opposed to merely receiving a laugh as a form of stylized tribute) would be disturbing, outside the proper order of things, as if the Statue of Liberty were to boom to the tourists: 'And here's another one!'

But America's most majestic human symbol over the past few years has been Ronald Reagan. Absolutely the most important point to remember about Reagan was that for eight years he had nothing much to do. Indeed, *doing* things wasn't what he was there for. His job was simply being. Take, for example, the time that a BBC crew went to tape a short interview with him for a programme about Margaret Thatcher.

The White House had warned them that they had exactly five minutes with the President, not a second more. He arrived on time in a cloud of aides, was briskly seated, and, as he talked, the various understrappers and hangers-on made signals indicating that the end of the interview was exceedingly nigh. The BBC people assumed that a crucial meeting to discuss the federal deficit was due, or Mr Gorbachev was on the line from Moscow. After precisely five minutes the aides wound it up and Reagan was ushered to the door, where he turned thoughtfully, and said: 'I just thought of an anecdote about Margaret Thatcher which I could tell you fellows. Do you have time?'

The BBC team were grateful, since almost nothing he had said up to that point had been much use at all. The aides looked panic-stricken. Reagan sat back in the seat and told the story, which was mildly amusing and appeared in the finished programme. Then he ambled off towards the door.

Before he got there, however, an American member of the crew politely handed him a letter which, he explained, had been written by his little daughter. He had promised to give it to the President. Instead of tucking it into his pocket, Reagan opened it on the spot and began to read something along these lines: 'Dear Mr President, I know you have a dog called Lucky. I have a dog called Trixie. Trixie is the same age as Lucky.' 'Why,' said Reagan, 'that means they're twins!'

The letter went on to say that Trixie was a naughty dog. Was Lucky? The little girl loved her dog. Did the President? Reagan read aloud with pleasure, chuckling his way through. The aides looked as if they were about to need by-pass surgery.

Finally they managed to get him out. Then twenty minutes later, as the crew were packing the last of their equipment, the aide who'd been left to supervise them said, between gritted teeth, as one might mutter, 'We thought Grandpop was in bed an hour ago': 'Why, look who's come back to see us!'

There in the doorway was the President, who asked who it was who had given him the letter from his little girl. He was glad to have caught them; it had taken him all this time in the Oval Office to find a photograph to sign, but here it was . . .

Many Americans to whom I told this story thought it very touching. In the middle of his hectic schedule, the President had taken time out to bring happiness to a small child. What they weren't to know was that there wasn't a busy schedule in the first place. Reagan had very little to do all day. Many of his (limited) waking hours were spent in personally answering his fan mail. Frequently he was fast asleep, a period known euphemistically as 'staff time', to the extent that during his election, parents would jokily call to their sleepy children: 'Come on in, honey, it's staff time.' Reagan was probably the first modern president to treat the post as a part-time job, one way of helping to fill the otherwise blank days of retirement.

He used to joke about it: 'They say hard work never killed anyone, but I figured, why take the chance?' Or, after a rare busy period, 'I've really been burning the midday oil.' The one-liners were meant to deflect criticism, and they succeeded, but they couldn't conceal the fact that they were true. The pretence that he was busy was a part of his prestige, as it is for many Americans in important positions. For his aides to have told the BBC, 'Yes, the President has all the time in the world', would have been the equivalent of his turning up at the Elysée Palace on a bicycle. In the same way, it is thought a mistake to return phone calls too quickly. Even if you have nothing better to do than riffle through your desk looking for photographs, it's crucial for your standing to keep people waiting a while.

The press and TV would occasionally talk about the President 'making a decision', which was a misuse of the term. Other presidents had staff whose job it was to assemble data and offer options. Reagan's people had the further task of providing him with decisions which he could ignore or, more usually, accept. He didn't *make* decisions; he *took* other people's decisions. They were the policy equivalent of oven-ready TV dinners, everything in its place, punch a button on the microwave and that's all you need to do. Staff who failed to make the decisions, and who presented him with lengthily argued on-the-one-hand, on-the-

201

other memoranda found themselves sacked, like Robert McFarlane. Reagan didn't dislike McFarlane; he just wished he would *tell* him less stuff.

Sometimes staff did not even bother to send the decisions up. The point about the Iran-Contra scandal was not that Reagan knowingly connived to divert funds. There's some evidence that, possibly, he might. But not a lot. After all, he didn't need to. He had people to do that, people who knew what he stood for, what he would have wanted if he had been bothered to think about it long enough to want it. Reagan was a flesh and blood version of any other mute national emblem, say the Statue of Liberty. Everyone knows what she represents, but no one would dream of asking her opinion. The scandal in the White House was not what Reagan knew but what nobody bothered to tell him.

Reagan instinctively understood the strength of American mythology. He also recognized, perhaps not consciously, that a myth is all the more powerful when it doesn't happen to be true. He mythologized his own life, imagining that he had served in the forces and had 'come home' after the war, when in fact, working on propaganda films, he had spent almost every night in his own bed. He said he had visited the German death camps, though he had actually only seen film of them. He believed that segregation in the armed forces had been ended by the courage of a black mess steward at Pearl Harbor, though this incident was only a scene in a film, and segregation continued to the end of the war. In Reagan's world, Hollywood speaks a deeper truth than reality ever can. It's well known that he used to make up phoney radio commentaries on baseball games, pretending he was at the stadium while actually reading the wire service ball-by-ball reports. But it's less well known that he gave demonstrations of this skill at the State Fair. People not only didn't mind him deceiving them; they liked it.

He had an artificial nickname invented for himself, 'The Gipper'. Even the story from which this derived was almost certainly faked, or at least a fable. George Gipp was the star player on the Notre Dame team trained by Knute Rockne, the most celebrated coach in football history. Reagan played Gipp in the film *Knute Rockne – All American* (even the title has a mythic quality: Rockne was actually born Norwegian, so the title glories in his apotheosis to Americanhood). Gipp died young but is alleged to have said to Rockne on his deathbed that, whenever the team was down at half-time and spirits were flagging, they should 'win one for the Gipper'. Reagan adopted this as his slogan, using it even on such banal occasions as a congressional vote. Yet Rockne was a notorious fantasist too, and there's no serious evidence that Gipp ever said any such thing. But so what? It's a myth, and a potent one too.

It's a rule of thumb that the most popular politicians are those who reflect a country's idea of itself back to itself. The British liked Churchill and, for a spell, Margaret Thatcher because they were tough, unyielding, leonine. These are not qualities which really mark us out as a nation, but we like to imagine that they do. The French like their leaders to possess tremendous dignity, as befits what is, in their view, the world centre of civilization. The Americans like someone who is amiable, easy-going, friendly and informal; slow to anger, but implacable when aroused. When Reagan left hospital after having had a malignant tumour removed, he thanked the doctors and nurses while wearing a baseball cap. It is inconceivable that President Mitterrand could appear in public wearing the French equivalent, say a jaunty beret. Neither he, nor any European leader, feels the need to appear as just another guy.

Europeans often thought of Reagan as a sabre-rattling bully, but that was never his style. Even after his military successes (for the most part, against weakling opponents such as Libya and Grenada) his tone was modest, more of sorrow than anger. The all-American hero is not Zorro, exultant over his enemies, but Shane, riding peaceably off into the setting sun, a distasteful job willingly if ruefully carried out.

It was the importance Reagan placed on being liked for which we can be grateful. His hatred of the Soviet system – which was sincere yet at the same time artificial; it was the myth he hated – did not survive his liking for Gorbachev. Reagan tended to believe anyone he liked, which is why he was so often let down by close colleagues such as Don Regan and John Poindexter. Gorbachev, for example, told him in Moscow that Jewish refuseniks were not permitted to leave the Soviet Union simply because of bureaucratic bungling. Not only did Reagan believe this nonsense, but repeated it several times, twice illustrating it with *Reader's Digest* anecdotes about similar bureaucratic ineptitude in America.

Yet this same simplicity – I use the term in both senses – also allowed him to believe that Gorbachev genuinely wanted to end the arms race. Reagan had several times wistfully wondered aloud how it would be if the earth were attacked by space aliens, and the superpowers were obliged to unite for the sake of the planet. This Buck Rogers fantasy clearly had a powerful appeal for him, and Gorbachev offered, if not the threat of flying saucers, at least the sense of unity and friendship. A more complicated and cautious man, like Bush, would have been much slower to seize the opportunity.

It's often pointed out that the American presidency involves two distinct jobs: head of government and ceremonial head of state. Certainly Reagan set more store by the latter task and put more effort into it. But an American head of state is not an uncrowned substitute for a king. Whereas even a constitutional monarch must preserve at least some aura, some mystique, if there is to be any point in his existence, his American equivalent has to strip all that away. Reagan, who was personally an aloof and somewhat distant man, never close to his friends, colleagues or even to his children, emotionally tied only to his wife, successfully contrived to appear on TV to look as if he wanted nothing better than to take all the voters on a fishing trip.

George Bush has tried to do the same thing, but in person rather than on television. In the early stages of his presidency it appeared that Bush hoped to meet every single American citizen, and give them each a puppy. I shook hands with him on the day after he had been inaugurated. He'd announced an open day at the White House. It was a revival of a custom which had ended in 1829 when visitors to Andrew Jackson's inaugural almost gutted the place, though in 1989 there were scores of security men waiting to make sure that didn't happen again. Bush first waved to the crowds from an upstairs window, then bounced down among them like Tigger. 'Let's scoot on in!' he cried merrily, as if the crowd of thousands was no more than a bunch of people he'd invited round for a barbecue.

The earliest to get into the house were greeted personally. 'Your first visit, how wonderful!' he said to one young man, 'it's good to see y'all, so glad you could come!' A woman had her hand pumped: 'Thank you for taking the time to stop by!', though since she was carrying her sleeping bag after a ten-hour wait, she could scarcely be said to have 'stopped by'. It's hard to dislike someone who is so desperately keen for you to like him.

He is a type one has often met; the fellow at the office who is painfully aware how dull he is, and makes up for it by unrelenting niceness. Somehow it's always his round, even when it isn't. The message is, 'Look, I don't expect you to find me amusing, or entertaining, or stimulating. But please like me, please don't leave me behind.'

I went to a party a few months after Bush was installed. It was a typical Washington do, at which all the guests spent their time slotting each other into mental Rolodexes. For instance, the reporter from the *Washington Post* didn't feel important enough to approach the Very Distinguished Columnist, but the VDC was happily swapping ironic remarks with the Extremely Famous Publisher.

Anyhow, there was a pause in the conversation and in, unannounced, walked President Bush. No one had said he was coming, no one had frisked us, and none of the handful of police outside had even asked to see our invitations. Bush shook hands with everyone present ('Good to meet you, heh heh, good to meet you'.) Nobody seemed surprised, or even particularly interested.

Soon afterwards there were short speeches. Bush talked for around a minute, then the Extremely Famous Publisher upstaged him with an orationette, thick with jokes, literary allusions and rhetorical curlicues. I looked over at Bush, who was standing under the lamp fixture, smiling vaguely and evidently wondering what to do with his hands. Lit from above, he was hard to recognize and might have been someone else altogether. I had the odd feeling that he had actually vanished, or perhaps hadn't been there in the first place, a sense only dispelled when I saw a picture of the event in *Time* magazine.

Bush does appear to lack that crucial charisma on an international scale. He seems to suffer from 'amsirac' which is (nearly) charisma spelled backwards. For us, amsirac means never getting a taxi in the rush hour, or waiting ten minutes while the barmaid finishes her conversation; for Bush it means that nobody much cares what you think about the future of Eastern Europe.

To some extent this is to do with important changes in the world. If one superpower, the Soviet Union, chooses to abdicate much of that role, then the authority of the rival superpower is necessarily undermined as well. If Cambridge announced that, owing to decades of failure, it was going to give up competing in the Boat Race, then who would care about the Oxford team?

But the problem is Bush's as well. All world leaders have celebrity *ex officio*, but some – such as Margaret Thatcher and Ronald Reagan – have it in their own right too. Bush does not. It's not only that the rest of the world worries a little less these days about what the United States thinks; but they find it hard to be too excited about what George Bush thinks.

Bush himself appears to be aware of this. Speaking at a black church in Washington, he said: 'Hey, I'm President of the United States. Can you believe it?' This is a strange remark, since the fact that George Bush is President is a matter of wonderment only to George Bush and his family. To the audience, the thing that might be hard to believe is the fact that any President at all has come to their church. But Bush is obsessed, deep down, with his own ordinariness. Flying to Paris on Air Force One, he was asked by a reporter, 'When did you first decide you were President? When did it hit you?' 'I don't know,' said Bush, 'but I'm deciding more and more that I am.'

'Bushisms' or 'Bush-speak' are by now world famous. Most of them do have an inner logic which you can either guess at, or else unravel from the context. Sometimes discerning what he means is like translating hieroglyphs: you do it by assuming roughly what he must mean, and so working out precisely what he does mean. Take the answer I heard him give, during the New Hampshire primary campaign, to a question about oil import taxes. This is the celebrated 'caribou' quotation:

'I'd like to see us open up that Alaska refuge, and that is important, because it was said once, remember when they built the pipeline, "Don't build the pipeline, you get rid of the caribou." The caribou love it, they rub up against it, and they have babies. There are more caribou in Alaska than you can shake a stick at.'

What he seems to mean here is that environmental considerations should not impede the search for oil. Or perhaps not.

Sometimes he refers to something which is familiar to him, but probably unknown to most of his listeners. Shortly before he went to visit President Reagan, he was asked whether he would take advice from his predecessor. He replied: 'Life its own self, as Dan Jenkins said. Life its own self. Figure that one out, Norm. But what it means is, I have a lot more to learn from President Reagan.' *Life Its Own Self* is a title of a book by Dan Jenkins, but its relevance to the topic remains obscure.

Occasionally Bush uses what appears to be family argot, or private family jokes. Once he was asked why he hadn't condemned violence against women while speaking to the National Rifle Association, and replied: 'Hey, listen, I'm a member of the NRA. You're hurting my feelings, as they say in China.'

Talking about the day's sport, he will say, for example, 'It was Vic Damone on the golf course today!' This means nothing more than that he won the game; 'Vic' is short for 'victory'. A tennis partner will be encouraged to smash by the phrase, 'Unleash Chiang!', an old anti-Communist war cry.

Often he misuses other people's slang. Early in his presidency the Bush dog, Millie, was about to give birth so Barbara Bush moved her into the marital bedroom, where her snuffles kept the President awake. He moved out. Asked how he felt about being driven from his bedroom by a dog, Bush said, 'It sure suits the heck out of me!'

It sometimes sounds as if he learned demotic speech through a Berlitz course; adequately but without any sense of what is fitting. After his debate with Geraldine Ferraro in 1984, he told longshoremen that he had 'kicked a little ass', which he must have thought was tough, guy talk, not realizing that it was wholly inappropriate in these (or just about any other) circumstances.

There seems to be something wrong with his inner ear. Angling for bone fish in Florida, he spotted some British tourists. 'How do you think Margaret Thatcher would like some of this *bone-fishing action*?' he yelled. The phrase sounds like some tremendous Australian euphemism.

His language falls to pieces fastest when he is under stress, for whatever reason. Here he is speaking to ghetto youths in Wilmington about the drug menace, necessarily a difficult *mise-en-scène* for any member of the white middle classes. He had been asked how he kept drugs out of his own life:

> 'Well, getting along in my level of life here, the pressures aren't quite that big. You don't have a lot of guys coming up to you in daily life, saying "Hey!" Now, like, I'm President. It would be pretty hard for some drug guy to come into the White House and start offering it up, you know? But I bet if they did, I hope I would say, "Hey, get lost! We don't want any of that!" '

Here's a field guide to some other famous Americans:

JAMES A. BAKER: If President Bush wants to be the nation's best friend, his Secretary of State is *his* best friend. Baker also has the job of being the unacceptable face of Bush. While the President goes in for the 'Shucks, I just wanna make everybody happy' act, Baker is the fellow who breaks the bad news in such a way as to make you feel worse. After the Tiananmen Square massacre, Baker made a cursory comment, then refused to say more, explaining: 'Now if you'll excuse us, we're very, very late for lunch.'

JIM BAKKER: disgraced diminutive TV evangelist, who leaves behind a baffling mystery. How come his name is written 'Bakker' when it's pronounced 'Baker'? At the time his empire collapsed, owning to the discovery of his liaison with Jessica Hahn, he was planning a life-size replica of the old Crystal Palace and theme park rides through Heaven and Hell, both based on the precise plans listed in the Book of Revelations.

TAMMY BAKKER: wife of the above, celebrated for never taking her make-up off, but allowing one coat to build up on another, like varnish. Subject of question: 'What will they find if they ever take off Tammy's make-up?' 'Jimmy Hoffa.'

CARL BERNSTEIN: half of the Woodward and Bernstein team which exposed Watergate. Having been played by Dustin Hoffman in the film of the scandal, he had an affair with Margaret Callaghan, daughter of the British Prime Minister, which was meant to be secret but was actually so well-known that it was broadcast on the tannoy at National Public Radio, where she worked at the time. The consequence was that Bernstein appeared in another film, this time of his wife's vengeful novel, and was played by Jack Nicholson. To be played by one famous star may be regarded as good fortune; to be played by two begins to look like impertinence.

JOE BIDEN: Democratic senator from Delaware, forced out of the 1988 presidential campaign when it turned out he had not only plagiarized a speech by Neil Kinnock, but had stolen Kinnock's life as well, making out that he was the son of impoverished miners. Has a pleasant but necessary line in self-deprecation, e.g. 'When I went back to my old school, the Dean told the leaving class that I reminded him of St Paul. I thought that sounded pretty nice. Then he went on, "Yes, St Paul, Minnesota, the most boring city in North America." '

ROBERT BORK: failed to be allowed to join the Surpeme Court after a long and successful campaign by liberal groups to keep him off, on the grounds that it is impossible to trust a man who has a beard but no moustache.

Bork has become a touchstone for right-wingers. On the same principle as the 'magic word' in the children's TV show *Pee-Wee's Playhouse*, it is obligatory at conservative functions, whenever Bork's name is invoked, to stand up and cheer.

PAT BUCHANAN: far right ideologue, formerly Ronald Reagan's director of communications. Now he is a columnist, but it is still Buchanan's job to produce an allegedly rational argument for indefensible ideas, e.g. the sale of ambassadorships to the person who gives most to campaign funds. Buchanan's next project: producing a coherent case for a return to child chimney sweeps.

WILLIAM F. BUCKLEY JR: right-wing thinker and publisher of the *National Review* who has modelled himself so closely on an English fogey that he is suspected of wearing tweed pyjamas. His distinctive, and almost impenetrable, speech is due to the fact that he breathes between syllables so sounds as if he is delivering dirty phone calls for intellectuals.

JIMMY CARTER: America's least popular post-war President, now regarded as its finest ex-President. There's a poignant display at his presidential library in Atlanta, Georgia, where through the miracle of laser discs, visitors are able to ask him why he didn't handle the hostage crisis better, and Carter, on a TV screen, tells them. It's an electronic plea: 'Hey, guys, could you have done better?'

JOAN COLLINS: star of *Dynasty*, celebrated for her energetic love life. Known in the US as 'The British Open'.

BILL COSBY: black entertainer and star of *The Cosby Show* which for years was the most popular programme on American TV. Cosby has set himself the task of endorsing every single product made in the United States. This has come to have a blackmailing effect: Cosby plugs so many things, that if he doesn't endorse yours, it must be really *terrible*.

MARIO CUOMO: Governor of New York, and the only full-time practising mystic in American politics today. Cuomo has dark nights of the soul the way that other governors have fund-raising breakfasts. When it comes time to decide whether to run for President in 1992, Cuomo is expected to consult his heroes, the late St Thomas More and Teilhard de Chardin, by ouija board before announcing another firm: 'Maybe.'

DALLAS: cast of: a dying breed. This is because its scriptwriters found a foolproof new way of saving money. When a star thought he or she had become indispensable and demanded 100,000 dollars an episode, they would read out an extract from the next series: 'Why, Pam, that plastic surgery you had following your terrible auto accident has completely changed you! I would never have recognized you!' 'Yeah. Those doctors gave me an *entirely new face*.' After that, they would generally settle for 20,000 dollars.

MICHAEL DEAVER: friend of Ronald Reagan's, who was so close to the 1980 Republican campaign that he kept a supply of different coloured watchstraps, so George Bush's could always tone with his suits. Deaver left the White House to become a millionaire lobbyist in direct contravention of the law, which states firmly that every pig must wait at least twelve months before being allowed to lower his snout into the gravy. Was convicted, but not jailed, the judge arguing that he had suffered enough. This is not a factor which has often been applied in sentencing youths who steal car radios.

SAM DONALDSON: White House correspondent for *ABC News*, and probably the only American to earn a good living entirely by shouting. It was his questions which Ronald Reagan spent years ignoring as he moved towards the WHUPP WHUPP of the helicopter. Reagan's departure meant that Donaldson was out of a job. An attempt to make him a popular co-host of a prime-time news show was not entirely successful.

MICHAEL DUKAKIS: Democratic candidate for President, 1988, now discredited Governor of Massachusetts. Most boring American to run for office since World War Two, hence the riddle: 'What's the difference between a Reagan cabinet and a Dukakis cabinet? The Reagan cabinet consists of twelve men wide-awake and one fast asleep; the Dukakis cabinet would be the other way round.' Dukakis once began a speech to a crowd in Texas with a joke, which he introduced by saying: 'The Latin scholars among you will appreciate this.'

ROBERT FULGHUM: America's best-selling non-fiction writer, author of *All I Really Need to Know I Learned in Kindergarten*, a collection of homely homilies in which Fulghum finds spiritual messages in everyday things, inspiration in a carburettor, sermons in stone-washed jeans. The title essay refers to being fair, sharing with your friends, taking afternoon naps and drinking milk. May be answered soon by a sceptics' version: *All I Really Need to Know I Learned in Business School*, e.g. buy short, sell long; always kick a man when he's down; avoid gilts.

ALBERT GORE: another Democratic candidate who, swept up in the furore over the judge who was prevented from joining the Supreme Court on the grounds that he had smoked pot, announced that he too had 'experimented with marijuana'. Other candidates, scared of future revelations, will no doubt soon admit to having 'experimented' with jay-walking, passing notes in class, and not leaving some for Mr Manners.

FAWN HALL: The thinking man's bimbo, America's equivalent of a Sloane Ranger. Though she was utterly loyal to her boss, Ollie North (she is said to have described their time together as 'shredded bliss'), it is regrettably not true that she stuffed her bra with secret documents in order to smuggle them out of the White House.

CHRISSIE HEFNER: daughter of Hugh Hefner, charged with rescuing the *Playboy* organization from near collapse. Since all the

213

men she meets tell her that they buy the magazine only for the articles about fine wines and world affairs, she is likely to attempt to double the circulation by removing all those pictures of naked women.

HUGH HEFNER: currently locked in a race with Donald Trump for the coveted title of America's Biggest Ego. Made a stunning bid for final supremacy in 1989 when he married Playmate Kimberley Conrad after putting out a $19.95 video of her naked body and a magazine entirely devoted to nude pictures of his bride-to-be.

JIM HIGHTOWER: Agriculture Commissioner in Texas, best known outside the State for his remark: 'If ignorance ever goes to forty dollars a barrel, I want drilling rights to George Bush's head.'

JESSIE JACKSON: may become the first black American politician to fall into the 'Oreo trap'. An Oreo is a cookie which is brown on the outside but white in the middle, and the term is used in the political trade for blacks who have succeeded by behaving in as 'white' a manner as possible. William Grey, a senior Democratic Congressman, and Doug Wilder of Virginia, America's first black Governor, are examples. They are acceptable to whites because they use the opposite of the old, haranguing, preacher style of oratory, which many whites associate with a threat to themselves.

Jackson has aimed straight for the white vote, with some success. He can win standing ovations from all-white audiences, especially in working-class areas. His celebrated routines ('How many of you got a VCR in your home? All of you stand. Now, all of you got a MX missile in your home, you stand! You see, we making things ain't nobody wants to buy!') are a thousand times funnier and more stirring than anything in American politics. Yet his tough rhetorical tone, his chanting, the pitch and swoop of his voice, all awaken hardly dormant fears among whites. It's not their culture, so it sounds like a threat to their culture. These days the successful black political image involves dressing like a lawyer and talking like an accountant.

HENRY KISSINGER: former Secretary of State and national security adviser who now appears on TV giving risible analyses of events abroad. Kissinger needs the publicity, since he now makes his money lending his name to multinational companies, who, questioned by anxious shareholders about the decision to build a chain of luxury hotels in Chad, can say: 'That's all right, we ran that one past Henry Kissinger.'

JOHN McLAUGHLIN: former priest, far right chairman of the TV show, *The McLaughlin Group*, in which equally far right people take turns to scream (a) at McLaughlin, and (b) at Jack Germond, the panel's token liberal. Unusual among American talk shows in that the participants actually hate each other *more* in real life than they appear to do on screen.

MADONNA: usually gorgeous, pouting young women with Rubensesque figures are principally admired by men. Madonna's fans are, however, young women and girls. What she is offering is a vision of adulthood which involves control (Madonna is always in charge) and which is every bit as much fun as childhood. In her sole film success, *Desperately Seeking Susan*, she liberates a bored and manipulated housewife who becomes like herself. In spite of (perhaps because of) her sassy manner and sexy underwear, Madonna's message to little girls is essentially reassuring and cosy: 'Look,' she says, 'it's going to be all right; you can still dress up and have a good time.'

RICARDO MONTALBAN: Mexican actor from the *Fantasy Island* TV series, now best known for advertising luxury Chrysler cars in an accent which would make a tamale curl. 'Peeble ask "Corinzian lezzer?" I say, "Of coss, wha'not zerr best?" ' It emerged that the phrase, 'Corinthian leather' has no meaning at all, apart from, possibly, 'leather'.

WALTER MONDALE: failed presidential candidate in 1984 who predicted that Reagan would get it all wrong. Was totally ignored at the time, and since, owning to the fact that − according to his wife − he had 'Norwegian charisma'. The humorist Mark Russell pointed out, 'So, if you think about it, does a sardine.'

PEGGY NOONAN: speech-writer for Ronald Reagan who wrote many of his most memorable lines before she even met him. Noonan ('Where do they find these men?', 'A thousand points of light') did for the President's oratory what flock wallpaper does for Indian restaurants. Later he published a set of his speeches, many written by her, the rest by other people, under the title: *Speaking My Mind*.

OLLIE NORTH: it is not often realized that North was deeply religious. Once he called an acquaintance about a colleague who was dying of cancer. Could he help? The man said he'd be delighted: money, babysitting the kids, flowers, anything he required. 'No,' said North, 'but we are having a series of prayer meetings on his behalf, and we'd like you to join.' The friend, an agnostic, refused. North used to arrive at informal parties in full-dress Marine uniform, and would spend hours fitting elaborate electronic equipment to his host's phone, so that he could call the White House situation room on a secure line.

North's wave of popularity in the summer of 1987, following his testimony to the Congressional Committee on the Iran-Contra affair, was one of the most short-lived crazes in American history, leaving the manufacturers of 'God Bless Colonel North' T-shirts with thousands of unsold stock. But it was enough at the time to terrify the Committee into submission, and may even have saved Ronald Reagan's presidency by making a real investigation of the scandal too politically perilous.

GENERAL COLIN POWELL: highest ranking black person ever in the US government, Powell left the White House to become Chairman of the Joint Chiefs of Staff. He had the smooth, practised patter of every administration official. I had a vision of him arriving at a press conference and, suddenly goaded beyond endurance, shouting at a reporter: 'Hey, my man, I want no more honky mo'fo' jive-ass from you!' But he never did.

JOAN QUIGLEY: San Francisco based astrologer who persuaded Nancy Reagan that she could predict good days and bad days for her husband. The good news was that she deemed the day Reagan was shot to be inauspicious. The bad news was that she didn't tell Nancy until after the event. Nancy signed her up anyway. Ms Quigley wrote a book claiming that, thanks to the stars, *she* had been able to bring about the end of the Cold War and to save the Reagan presidency. After the San Francisco earthquake, a reporter phoned Ms Quigley and asked if she had predicted it. She explained that she didn't do earthquakes.

DAN RATHER: weird CBS newsreader, the highest paid in the US, who once signed off a bulletin with the single word 'Courage', for no apparent reason. Once said he had been beaten up in a New York street by two men who kept asking him: 'Kenneth, what is the frequency?', giving rise to speculation that they were either space aliens, or else thought that he was. Watch Rather on TV at night and observe a strange fact: his eyes follow you round the room.

NANCY REAGAN: the loopiest First Lady since Mary Todd Lincoln. She would appear in fabulously expensive designer couture to pass on her anti-drugs 'Just Say No' message to ghetto youths, even while her husband was cutting funds to the Coast Guard. With Ronnie, preached the virtues of family, religion and hard work, though at least one of her own children couldn't stand her, the Reagans almost never went to church, and liked to be in their pyjamas at 6 p.m.

PAT ROBERTSON: TV preacher and Republican candidate for President, who claimed to have diverted a hurricane round his Virginia headquarters by the power of prayer. Promised that if he became President, he would arrange for bright sunny weather turning to partly cloudy later in the day, with a chance of showers towards nightfall, so don't forget your umbrella.

ANDY ROONEY: professional curmudgeon, allowed on CBS to give gruff, no-holds-barred pieces to camera on controversial topics such as 'Why do we always leave umbrellas behind?' and 'Whatever happens to those single socks which get lost in the laundry?' When Rooney did say something genuinely debatable, about whether poor people diluted their genes by having too many children, he was suspended without pay.

JEFF SMITH: the Frugal Gourmet. Immensely popular TV cook who describes how to take a set of disgusting, almost inedible ingredients, and miraculously whisk them up into a disgusting, almost inedible meal. Great to watch if you have a freezer full of turkey gizzards and beetroot.

HOWARD STERN: America's first Zen disc jockey, whose gimmick is to play no music at all. Instead his show consists entirely of extremely sick jokes interspersed with whingeing complaints to a woman companion, mainly about the Federal Communications Commission which has received innumerable complaints about his show. This mixture has made him the most popular broadcaster in the nation's biggest city, New York.

ROBERT STRAUSS: *Éminence* extremely *grise* of the Democratic Party and thought to be the second most powerful person in Washington, after Mrs Katherine Graham. Strauss is the man who, asked what the Democrats should do to win an election, declared: 'We need a candidate who, when he walks down the corridor, you can hear his balls clank.'

JIMMY SWAGGART: another TV preacher, who was caught out with a prostitute in a New Orleans motel so sleazy that you had to call room service to have the Gideon Bible sent up.

DONALD TRUMP: now embattled multi-millionaire property

developer in New York City engaged in a toe-to-toe fight with Hugh Hefner for the title of America's Greatest Ego. He prefers to use gold leaf instead of wallpaper, and if he knew what frankincense and myrrh were, he'd slap them on the walls too. Garry Trudeau of 'Doonesbury' suggests that Trump's final act of self-admiration will be to name himself after himself, 'Trump J. Trump – the name screams quality'.

BARBARA WALTERS: TV interviewer who has parlayed a speech defect and an insatiable curiosity about other people's sex lives into a multimillion-dollar career. Her show has become a version of the confessional box, and her principal aim is to make her interviewee cry. A typical Walters interview goes something like this:

Barbara: in the studio tonight, to talk about the collapse of Communism and the pwospects fow a more peaceful world, Soviet pwesident Mikhail Gorbachev.

Gorbachev: Hi, Barbara.

Barbara: Mike, have you ever been unfaithful to Raisa?

(Gorbachev breaks down in great sobs.)

Afterword

Shortly after writing this book, and six months after leaving our home in the US, I returned for a visit. The country changes itself with extraordinary speed. When I left in 1989, the States were far behind Europe in concern for the environment. Not a single car sported a green plastic nose, there was no Ben Elton figure to tell eco-sensitive jokes on prime-time TV, warnings about disposable nappies were seen largely as the work of cranks.

In half a year they had streaked ahead of us, as if the nation had a turbo-charged psyche. 'Earth Day' on 20 April 1990 dominated every newspaper and magazine. Just as every product had proclaimed 'Contains oat bran' on the packet (including some, I suspect which you weren't even supposed to eat), now they declared 'Recyclable' instead. The first place I went to, Boulder, Colorado, has always been ecologically minded, but now people seemed to talk of little else. Posters around town called on the Mitsubishi Corporation to lay off the Indonesian rain forests. Signs appeared in bookshops: 'For ecological reasons, we do not supply bags unless asked', while a few feet away people were undoing all that good work by throwing away several pounds of newsprint, the unwanted sections from the vast Sunday newspapers.

They've always talked about the 'fragile' Rocky Mountains in Boulder, rather as if they were a set of cheap bathroom shelves. They're fidgety about people walking on them, like housewives fretting over the new sitting-room carpet. But the mood is growing bossier. Now that preserving the high meadows is thought important, we can soon expect to see signs abjuring us to take off our shoes before walking on the mountain.

There are now more nuclear-free zones, not only in the hope that enemy missiles would miss Eugene, Oregon, and Takoma Park, Maryland, but so that local police can be banned from spending public money on goods from any company which has ever had any links with nuclear contractors. (On the whole, however, the environment is replacing the threat of nuclear war as the Principal Cause of Underlying Anxiety. We in the prosperous West like having something to worry about. Go to Third World countries and you will often hear people being bouncy and hopeful, because they require a degree of optimism to survive. We, with our comfy homes, well-stocked stores and healthy children, seem to need something to dread.)

We tend to laugh at their excesses, but it's all part of the American determination to succeed. There's a job which requires doing, which is preserving the planet. So we must do whatever is necessary until the task is accomplished. I sometimes suspect that the obsessive desire for sporting triumph, instilled at a ludicrously early age, is important here. It may seem nonsensical to insist on victory in sport, since inevitably each event is going to end in failure for someone. Yet this also teaches another lesson: that setbacks are only temporary. A loss is not a defeat, only a preparation for the vital task of winning next time.

I'd hate to be a politician who got in the way of this force. George Bush might be doing his best, but I can't see him surviving long in the role of polluters' friend. Meanwhile, the President is beginning to seem even more transparent, fading and reappearing in the national consciousness. Like Wells's Invisible Man he, one suspects, wears clothes only in order to be seen, and makes speeches only in order to appear to have something to say. Those around him, such as his Secretary of State James Baker and his Chief of Staff John Sununu, seem by contrast as solid as Mount Rushmore. Bush exists mainly as a reflection of his poll ratings.

I noticed another national mood swing had occurred. Ronald Reagan, who in 1989 left office in a blaze of, if not glory, at least amiable approval, had become – according to his polls – the least regarded ex-president of modern times. His two-million-dollar speaking tour of Japan (which has taken on the Soviet Union's

221

role as Chief National Opponent); the bickering about just how much use he made of Ms Joan Quigley, the San Francisco astrologer whom Nancy Reagan admits to having consulted and who claims to have been pretty much running all global affairs since 1981; and Reagan's unseemly inability to help John Poindexter, his national security adviser during the Iran-Contra scandal – all these tragi-farcical events have made Americans see Reagan now in much the same way as the rest of the world has for years. The pendulum swings slowly but certainly; in two years' time he may be reassessed as the greatest Chief Executive since Roosevelt. Or perhaps it will take much longer.

There had been lesser changes too. The Sixties were back in fashion. Men wore pigtails. Clothes shops sold out of tie-dyed shirts. This was attributed to the end of the Reagan 'greed-head' era, though I don't think Americans were particularly greedy then. The greedy minority were, however, highly visible.

Donald Trump was in trouble, though his planes had indeed been redecorated in high-tech camp, as if Norman Foster had designed a bordello. Apart from the lack of gold seat-belt buckles, the Trump fleet, with its leather seating, chrome trim and pink marble bathrooms, was actually more kitsch than Elvis Presley's old plane, the *Lisa Marie*.

As if in answer to criticisms of Amtrak, the national passenger rail service, someone had started a luxury train running between Chicago, Washington and New York. Instead of sitting in a mock aeroplane, you are in a lavishly appointed club car, and sip champagne while the desperate slums of Chicago glide past. It is actually more luxurious than any American train that ever existed, except for private ones, and so perfectly captures an important element of the nation: you recreate the past, but you recreate it much better than it was.

Similarly there is a theme park in Virginia called Busch Gardens, which includes a section called 'Europe'. Except that this vision of the Old World is better than the real thing, being cleaner, English-speaking, and generally free of crime. People think such things are phoney, and they are. Yet this misses the point. There is American innocence, the belief that you *can* go to, say, Rome, without risking your purse or encountering any unpleasant odours. Or London, and still find a decent hot dog.

Places like this, though, are not a substitute for experience, but an improvement on it. They *are* the real thing, only better. I sometimes suspect that this phrase might make a good epitaph for the whole of the United States, the country which invented itself, and can't stop tinkering with the result.